R.A. Huelsmann

LAND OF THE GIANTS

A History of Minnesota Business
by Don W. Larson

Published by Dorn Books
7101 York Ave. South
Minneapolis, MN 55435

Creative Supervisor: Kenneth M. Nelson
Art Director: Sherry Reutiman

First Edition
First Printing 1979
ISBN 0-934070-03-2

PREFACE

We believe that readers of this book will discover that the business history of Minnesota is a fascinating, colorful and varied story. From the early days of lumber, iron ore and milling industries and the men who founded them, through more modern entrepreneurs and businessmen of recent decades, there are many tales of hard work, good and bad luck, financial panics and depressions, determination, and daring. The contributions of Minnesota business and industry to the nation's World War II efforts and the state's recent role as a leading computer, electronics and medical devices center are also covered. All in all, it is a rich panorama.

Peat, Marwick, Mitchell & Co. has had offices in the Twin Cities for 75 of the years that are covered in this history. As part of observing our 75th anniversary we commissioned this volume, authored by Don W. Larson. Mr. Larson is Senior Editor of CORPORATE REPORT magazine, a very highly regarded monthly magazine covering business in the Upper Midwest—more specifically, the Ninth Federal Reserve District.

We think Don Larson has done an outstanding job, and would like to offer him our congratulations.

We think you will agree.

The Minneapolis and St. Paul offices of Peat, Marwick, Mitchell & Co.

TABLE OF CONTENTS

Chapter 1

It's difficult to fully appreciate the interesting and colorful history of business ventures in Minnesota without first scrutinizing the present. None of those hardy entrepreneurs of a century ago, who struggled and toiled to establish businesses in the Minnesota backwoods, while the real action was more than a thousand miles to the east, could have even dreamed that, by the 1980s, the state would be a leading industrial center—not only in the nation, but in the world. Despite the fact that Minnesota was settled 100 years after commerce had a healthy start in the eastern part of the United States, a combination of unusual factors has resulted in relatively rapid growth of successful business activity in this rather isolated Midwestern state.

Where does Minnesota presently rank among all 50 states relative to business? Dozens of statistical studies measure industrial vitality in the country, but one of the most interesting indexes may be obtained simply by looking at the real giant corporations to see where they were started and where they are presently headquartered. In the United States today, there are about 550 companies with annual sales (or assets) in excess of a billion dollars. These include publicly held corporations, private companies, cooperatives and mutual companies, such as certain insurance firms. If these were divided equally among all states, there would be 11 in each state. If they were distributed according to population, the most populous states, California and New York, would each have 50 of these giant companies, while Minnesota and each of the other 30 sparsely settled states would have a single billion-dollar business. The others would be scattered among the remaining 17 bigger states.

In actuality, these behemoths of the business world are not distributed in any orderly fashion, and most are located where they were founded and allowed to grow from tiny enterprises to the giants they are today. California, for instance, with 52 of the billion-dollar companies headquartered there, has just about the number it should have, according to population. But Illinois, with the dynamic Chicago area acting like a magnet, has 55 of these big corporations, even with half of California's population. And New York, the business capital of the world, has 123, more than double any other state.

What about Minnesota? With fewer than four million people within its boundaries, ranking 19th among all states in population, Minnesota is headquarters for 24 companies doing more than a billion dollars apiece in annual sales, or with assets exceeding that figure. With only 1.7 percent of the country's population, Minnesota has 4.4 percent of the nation's biggest businesses. In addition, at least five others in the billion-dollar category were founded here, but, for one reason or another, left to establish headquarters in other states.

The most famous of the five emigrants is Sears, Roebuck & Co., which was founded in Minneapolis in 1886 by Richard Sears as the R.W. Sears Watch Co. As a railroad stationmaster at Redwood Falls, Minn., Sears had obtained a large number of watches from his unclaimed freight. He sold the timepieces by mail through a business he formed in Minneapolis. The venture was so successful he expanded into other lines and moved to Chicago, where he took Alvah Roebuck as a partner. The former stationmaster's idea is now the largest retailing chain in the country, with close to $20 billion in annual sales.

Nearly as famous is the Greyhound Corp., which was founded in 1915 at Hibbing, Minn., as the Mesaba Transportation Co. It is now based at Phoenix, Ariz., and has annual revenues of more than $4 billion. About the same size is the diversified wood-products concern, the Weyerhaeuser Corp., founded by the Minnesota lumber king, Frederick Weyerhaeuser, who came to St. Paul in 1891 and soon thereafter formed the Weyerhaeuser Timber Co., which grew into the largest operation of its kind before moving its headquarters to Tacoma, Wash., after Minnesota's prime forests had been depleted. The other two Minnesota-born giants, both approaching $2 billion in sales a year, are Archer-Daniels-Midland, founded in Minneapolis at the turn of the century and now located at Decatur, Ill., and Gould, Inc., which had its start in St. Paul as Gould National Batteries. Now a diversified conglomerate, Gould moved to Rolling Meadows, Ill., a decade ago.

Depending on the kind of activities involved, industrialization can have widely varying positive and negative effects on an area. Fortunately, Minnesota has, over the years, attracted primarily so-called clean businesses and has escaped most of the adverse by-products of heavy industry. The state has its steel mills, oil refineries and foundries, but these are not the main activities in Minnesota. Food companies, computer manufacturers, transportation companies, diversified manufacturers, financial institutions, big retailers and insurance firms dominate the business community here.

A healthy business community reflects itself in many ways. First of all, successful businesses provide jobs. Minnesota's unemployment rate historically ranks lower than the average in the country, and in the mid-1970s, during the most severe recession in the U.S. since the 1930s, the jobless rate here was only half that of the national average.

Successful businesses are also financially rewarding to their owners, investors and key managers. Evidence of this can be found in Minnesota by counting the number of millionaires. A nationwide study conducted in 1979 by the United States Trust Co. of New York showed that Minnesota has 5.7 millionaires for every 1,000 residents, a record that is exceeded in only four other states. The survey counted 22,873 Minnesotans with a net worth of more than a million dollars.

People with wealth normally are generous in their contributions to charitable and cultural organizations, and such groups have had exceptional support in Minnesota over the years. It's not only wealthy individuals, however, who funnel money into worthwhile organizations in Minnesota. The state has been a leader in corporate donations. Under federal tax laws, a corporation is allowed to deduct up to five percent of its pre-tax income in charitable contributions. According to a study done in 1978 by the *New York Times,* there were 37 corporations in the United States giving the full five percent to charity. Of those 37 companies, an overwhelming 33 of them are headquartered in Minnesota. The Minnesota Corporate Community Five-Percent Investment Club, formed in 1976, has given the state an edge in a growing national trend toward increased corporate charity. Throughout the country, the average amount donated by corporations has been running less than one percent. The amount in Minnesota, primarily because of the Five-Percent Club, is averaging nearly double that figure. And, though the five-percent philosophy is relatively new, even in Minnesota, several firms in the state have been pledged to this practice for years. Dayton Hudson, the Minneapolis-based retailer, has been giving five percent of its pre-tax earnings to charitable, educational and community programs for 32 years.

Another important by-product of a vigorous business community is the role it plays in the overall quality of life for all of an area's residents. In several studies, all conducted within the past decade, Minnesota has ranked either first or close to the top on quality-of-life scales. The criteria in these surveys vary, of course, but they normally include state and local expenditures for education per capita, the number of higher educational institutions, the number of doctors and dentists per 100,000 population, the number of hospital beds per 1,000 population, the percent of owner-occupied homes, expenditures per capita on parks and recreation and money spent on the arts. In each of these categories, Minnesota ranks extremely high, usually in the top five.

The emphasis on quality of life, which suggests that Minnesotans live better, is perhaps one reason why Minnesotans also live longer. In a recent survey, the state ranked second, next to Hawaii, in life expectancy.

In scrutinizing the present state of affairs of the business community, it would not be fair to emphasize only the positive aspects. Like all states, Minnesota has its problems, some of them more severe than its neighbors.

One problem, which doesn't seem to have any near-term solution, is the swallowing up of large numbers of Minnesota-based companies through acquisitions by larger firms from other states and countries. Through such purchases, Minnesota doesn't always "lose" these companies, but it does lose the advantages of having these firms headquartered in the state. Outside ownership more often than not works to the disadvantage of the citizens of the state. The magnitude of the problem probably can be demonstrated by the fact that in just a two-year period (1977 and 1978) Minnesota lost more than 50 home-grown corporations to firms headquartered in other states. The companies sold had a total value exceeding $2 billion.

Now it's true that Minnesota corporations also are acquiring firms—many of them outside the state. For instance, in that same two-year period, Minnesota companies bought 118 firms elsewhere. But the pattern seems to show Minnesota losing its bigger companies while adding mostly smaller firms. The 118 corporations added to Minnesota ownership had a total value of only $1.3 billion compared to the $2 billion involved in the companies sold. And, while this book was being prepared for publication, Minnesota was losing the ownership of one of its billion-dollar companies, Investors Diversified Services, to a New York-based firm, Allegheny Corp. Other large Minnesota corporations which have been sold to out-of-state buyers in recent years include Hoerner Waldorf, Data 100, Northrup King, Fingerhut, Cardiac Pacemakers, Minnesota Title, Blandin Paper, Rosemount, Ridder Publications, Campbell-Mithun Advertising, Miller Publishing, Creamette Co., Coca Cola Midwest and Aslesen's. Dozens of smaller concerns have also been acquired.

While the majority of purchases by Minnesota companies has been of smaller firms, there have been some notable exceptions. Cargill, for instance, added a billion-dollar company with its 1979 purchase of the MBPXL Corp., a Wichita, Kan., meat-packing firm with 1978 sales of $1.3 billion. And even though Minnesota lost the Green Giant company through acquisition in 1979, it went to another Minneapolis corporation, Pillsbury.

But, all in all, merger activity poses a threat to the future of Minnesota's business vitality.

An equally serious problem, but one which will probably correct itself, is the loss of publicly held companies. This situation, which is due to an adverse investment climate, currently prevails, however, in all states. Minnesota has seen more than 300 publicly held corporations disappear—for a variety of reasons—in the past 10 years and has had only a handful of new firms come on the scene to replace them. Back in the late 1960s, it was not uncommon to see four or five new companies "go public" every week. In the 1970s, that rate has dwindled to only four or five a year. The main reason, of course, is the rapid decline of investment capital. Fluctuation in the availability of venture capital has been cyclical historically, so it's safe to assume that sometime in the near future investors will once again be willing to put money into the formation of new businesses and that, naturally, will benefit not only Minnesota, but all states.

A third problem, one that is peculiar to Minnesota but one which shows signs of being corrected to some extent, is the unfavorable business climate caused mostly by a state legislature that for a dozen years has been less than friendly to business interest. With a whopping 12-percent rate, Minnesota has the dubious distinction of having the highest state corporate income tax in the nation. The state also has one of the country's highest state personal income tax rates for people in top income brackets. Its workmen's compensation laws have been punitive to business, and its estate and inheritance taxes have encouraged wealthy retired businesspeople to leave the state. Minnesota has had, until 1979, a discriminatory tax on railroads, but this, along with some of the other problems, is being corrected. The trend in Minnesota, as the 1980s begin, is to make the state once again attractive for business.

Because of the size of leading businesses here, overall corporate health hasn't appeared to suffer from adverse public policy. It's only when you look at the small-to-medium-sized businesses that you find trouble signs. Most of these troubles begin to pale, however, when they are considered alongside the overwhelming positive aspects of the state's business scene. Without question, the healthiest factor, next to the sheer size of the companies involved, is the remarkable diversification of the industries operating in Minnesota. No single industry dominates the scene, and this nicely protects the state when the inevitable downturns hit particular segments of our society.

The nearly recession-proof food industry, firmly entrenched here because of Minnesota's strong agricultural base, is one of the chief factors in the state's economic stability. Six of the state's billion-dollar companies, including three of the top five, are involved in food in one way or another. Cargill, the largest company in Minnesota measured in sales and profits (and the largest privately held corporation in the United States), is the world's biggest grain trader, getting about half of its annual $12.6 billion in revenues in 1978 from that activity. Cargill also is involved in corn milling, soybean processing, meat packing, salt mining, poultry processing and animal feeds. Its non-food activities include steel manufacturing, chemicals and insurance. Cargill employs 25,000 workers.

General Mills, the state's fourth largest concern, has evolved over the years from a flour miller to a highly diversified firm with heavy emphasis on food processing and restaurants. Its $3.3 billion in sales and 67,000 employees make it one of the state's most important companies.

Minnesota's fifth largest company, Super Valu, also is engaged in the food business but from another direction. It is the country's largest food wholesaler, supplying 2,000 retail stores, including more than 100 of its own. It also is diversified into such things as clothing (200 County Seat stores in 33 states), department stores, insurance, architectural design and store engineering and interior design.

Another former flour-milling giant, the Pillsbury Co., has, like General Mills, diversified into a food conglomerate. The 15th largest food processor in the nation, Pillsbury has about 40 percent of its assets tied up in facilities for the eating-out crowd. It has nearly 2,000 Burger King outlets, plus Steak & Ale and Poppin' Fresh restaurants. Half the size of General Mills, Pillsbury shows signs of healthy growth in the future. Its 1979 acquisition of Green Giant, a half-billion-dollar (annual sales) Minnesota corporation, was a big step in that direction.

The strong cooperative movement here, paced by Land O'Lakes, is also a vital factor in Minnesota's food industry. The

Minneapolis-based regional farm supply and food marketing concern, is owned by more than 850 local co-ops and 12,000 direct member-patrons. With its 1978 purchase of Spencer Foods, Inc., a Spencer, Iowa, meat packer, Land O'Lakes became a $2-billion operation with more than 200 milk, poultry, feed and other farm-related plants in Minnesota, Wisconsin, North Dakota, South Dakota, Iowa and Nebraska.

Not far behind Land O'Lakes in size is the Farmers Union Grain Terminal Association (GTA), one of the largest grain handlers in the United States. It operates more than 600 elevators, eight terminals, oil-seed processing plants, malt plants, feed plants, durum mills and more than 100 lumber yards.

A third major cooperative, the South St. Paul-based Farmers Union Central Exchange (CENEX), just barely misses the billion-dollar-a-year category. It serves more than 1,200 other cooperatives supplying nearly 400,000 farmers in 10 states. Midland Cooperatives, Inc., is another large Minnesota supplier. plier.

Although regarded as a general retailing firm, Gamble Skogmo is heavily involved in the food industry through its ownership of Red Owl Stores, Inc., which has nearly 400 supermarkets. The food business contributes nearly 40 percent of Gamble's $1.5 billion in annual sales.

The last of the state's billion-dollar food-industry giants is the only one based outside the Twin Cities area. The Geo. A. Hormel Co., a meat packer, is headquartered at Austin, in southern Minnesota. It has plants throughout the Midwest.

Four other Minnesota firms in the food business will most likely be in the billion-dollar category before the 1980s are over. These are International Multifoods, Nash Finch, Pacific Gamble Robinson and Peavey. Not far behind are Jeno's, Applebaum's Food Markets, International Dairy Queen, Sunstar Foods, Marshall Foods and Robel Beef.

Dozens of other food companies based in Minnesota, are doing more than a million dollars a year in sales. They include American Fruit and Produce, American Crystal Sugar, Bongards Creameries, Butterfield Foods, Elliott Packing, Ewald Brothers, Fritz, M.A. Gedney, L.B. Hartz, Home Produce, Jack Frost, Jennie-O-Foods, Landy Packing, Meat Distributors, North Star Foods, Northland Milk, Old Dutch Foods, Owatonna Canning, Pan-O-Gold Baking, Processed Potatoes, Sather Cookie, Stewart Infrared, Superior Dairy, Wadco Foods and Willmar Poultry.

These are just the companies headquartered in Minnesota. Hundreds of food companies that belong to firms based elsewhere also operate in the state.

Agriculture and the food industry it spawned stretches back to the earliest days of Minnesota's business history and, for that reason, commands a unique position. But for glamour, color and excitement you must turn to a much newer industry, one that promises to do for the 20th Century what railroading did for the 19th. This is, of course, the computer field. While most people equate computers with IBM—and well they should, for this New York-based company makes about six of every 10 computers sold—the industry was actually born in Minnesota and in reality, International Business Machines is just a Johnnie-come-lately.

It was in those hectic days just after World War II that two-dozen brainy Minnesotans, working out of a quonset hut in St. Paul's Midway District, built the first commercial computer, opening up what probably will be the century's most important industry. And though IBM is presently dominating the field, Minnesota still ranks as one of the top three or four computer centers in the United States. One of every six workers in U.S. computer hardware factories is a Minnesotan, and 12 cents of every dollar's worth of computers produced in the country come from Minnesota.

The importance of the computer age in Minnesota can perhaps best be measured by the fact that nearly 40,000 workers are employed by the industry in the state. About 170 Minnesota corporations, nearly 90 producing computers, components or peripheral equipment and another 80 in the software field, are involved.

Of the world's five largest computer manufacturers, three were founded in Minnesota and four of them, including IBM, have major facilities in the state. IBM's Rochester, Minn., plant employs more than 4,000 workers. Univac, the earliest entry in the field and the company given the credit for developing the industry, was founded in St. Paul. The company later was sold to Sperry Rand and is now a division of the parent, but the bulk of its computer business is still located in Minnesota, and more than 11,000 people earn their living here with this pioneer. Honeywell and Control Data, two others in the Big Five, were both founded in Minnesota and have remained here. Honeywell is an old-time firm which evolved into computers, but Control Data was formed just for the purpose of making these electronic wizards. It is probably the only corporation in history to have gone from zero sales to more than

$2 billion annually in just 20 years.

Of course, the entire computer industry, compared to other fields, has experienced such explosive growth that it's difficult to comprehend. In the 20 years following the introduction of the computer called Univac I in 1953, the industry grew to 30 times its original size. This phenomenal growth has tapered off as the industry has matured, and, in contrast to expectations in the late 1960s, Minnesota has not garnered exclusive rights to the field. It remains, however, an important part of the state's business community.

A field that is equally as vital to Minnesota as food and computers is diversified manufacturing. The best example is Minnesota Mining and Manufacturing Co., or the 3M Co., as it prefers to be known. The second largest corporation in Minnesota, 3M has $4.7 billion in worldwide sales a year and a system-wide payroll of 85,000 workers, about the same as Honeywell.

It's hard to describe the nature of 3M's business because of the vast number of products it makes. With 45 major product lines, 3M manufactures literally thousands of different items, ranging from 600 kinds of tape to dozens of office machines. It has major plants in 93 communities in 32 states. With 22,000 employees in Minnesota alone, 3M is not only a significant factor in the state's economy, but along with firms like Honeywell and Control Data, it gives this area worldwide impact. 3M has facilities in 50 foreign countries on six continents.

Corporations such as 3M make it obvious why Minnesota has such an abnormal number of millionaires. Many of the company's 123,000 shareholders live in the state, and owning stock in 3M has produced more wealth than is commonly realized for a large number of Minnesotans. When the company was formed in 1902 and for many years thereafter, 3M stock was often taken in lieu of wages by workers for the struggling firm. A block of 100 original shares of 3M, nearly worthless 80 years ago, had a value of $2.3 million in 1979.

And while 3M is one of the better known manufacturing firms in Minnesota, it is only one of hundreds in the state. To put 3M in better perspective, you only have to weigh its 22,000 workers in the state against the more than 300,000 Minnesotans earning their livings from manufacturing.

Not as significant as manufacturing from an economic standpoint, but an industry which has been important to the state since its very beginning is transportation. Two of Minnesota's billion-dollar giants, Burlington Northern and Northwest Airlines, lead this industry, but, as in all other fields, there are dozens of transportation companies making valuable contributions.

No single industry has been more important in making it possible for Minnesota to become a vital area for commerce. Originally, it was the natural waterways that opened the state, but railroads came in during the 1860s to dominate travel in and out of the state, and, as the demands of the 20th Century increased, airplanes and trucks filled the void. Today, the intricate web of transportation available in Minnesota is as vital to the state's growth as the railroads were 100 years ago.

Since the end of World War II, the mushrooming growth of the commercial airlines has highlighted transportation developments, and because of Minnesota's role as a business center, that growth has been especially notable here. In fact, two of the nation's dozen biggest commercial airlines, Northwest Airlines and the new Republic Airlines, are headquartered in Minnesota. Northwest began as a contract mail carrier in 1926 and carried its first passenger a year later. Republic was formed in 1979 when Minneapolis-based North Central Airlines purchased Southern Airlines.

Nearly all of the other large air carriers have major terminals at the Minneapolis-St. Paul International Airport, the 16th busiest airport in the country. The Twin Cities facility is unusual in that its location, unlike that of most major airports, is right in the heart of the metropolitan area—just eight miles from both downtown Minneapolis and downtown St. Paul. The value of air transportation in keeping Minnesota a vital business center is immeasurable.

Less glamorous now but once just as romantic as the airlines and still equally important to the overall industrial picture, are the state's railroads. Home base for the country's largest railroad in terms of miles of track, Minnesota has been an important railroad center almost since statehood in 1858. Burlington Northern was formed in 1970 by the merger of Great Northern Railroad, the Northern Pacific and a couple of smaller companies. The company has one of the most interesting and tumultuous histories of any Minnesota business. It is not the only large railroad based in the state, however. The bustling Soo Line Railroad Co., formed in 1961 through the merger of three railroads, is an important freight hauler, too. In addition, three other railroads—Chicago & Northwestern, Chicago Milwaukee St. Paul & Pacific and the Minneapolis, Northfield & Southern—serve the state. Another 38 railroad companies have offices in Minnesota.

Burlington Northern, although known primarily as a railroad, is also heavily involved in natural resources and the air-freight business and is an important element in Minnesota's trucking industry.

Because no single firm dominates the truckers, the fact that Minnesota is one of the liveliest trucking centers in the country often goes unnoticed. Its location midway between the East Coast and the West Coast, and its proximity to Chicago, has helped Minnesota grow in importance for trucking, but the field is scattered with nearly 20 large common carriers and hundreds of independent truckers based here.

Some of the larger Minnesota trucking firms include Briggs Transportation, Murphy Motor Freight Lines, Werner Continental, Advance-United Expressways, Anderson Trucking, Admiral-Merchants Motor Freight, Berger Transfer and Storage, Century-Mercury Motor Freight, Dahlen Transport, Glendenning Motorways, Indianhead Truck Lines, La Salle Cartage, Minnesota-Wisconsin Truck Line, Nationwide Carriers, Quickie Transport and United Van Bus Delivery.

A field which has both giants and a host of small entrepreneurs is retailing. Dayton Hudson and Gamble Skogmo, two of the largest retailers in the United States, are based in the Twin Cities. Both started from scratch and have seen spectacular growth, especially in recent years. Both are diversified and big employers of Minnesota workers.

The large number of financial institutions headquartered in Minnesota really surprises most out-of-state visitors. Why an isolated state so far away from the money-centers of the East should have eight multi-billion-dollar financial and insurance firms is a perplexing question. The answer, of course, is that each started here as a small enterprise with no thought of growing into the mammoth institutions they eventually became, and none found a good enough reason to move from the area.

Two of the country's largest bank holding companies, each with assets of about $10 billion, are Northwest Bancorporation and the First Bank System. Both are headquartered in downtown Minneapolis but have tentacles stretching throughout the Midwest. Investors Diversified Services, an unusual financial-services company based in Minnesota since its formation in 1894, owns or manages more than $8 billion in assets for more than two million customers. Controlling ownership was transferred to a New York company in 1979, but the headquarters remain in Minneapolis.

Two of the nation's largest savings and loan associations are also headquartered in Minnesota. They are Twin City Federal Savings and Loan and Midwest Federal Savings and Loan. And Minnesota is home for three of the nation's largest insurance companies—the St. Paul Companies, Minnesota Mutual and Northwestern National Life.

Minnesota is also the home for one of the largest fraternal insurance organizations in the United States, Lutheran Brotherhood Life Insurance Society. Lutheran Brotherhood with over 8 billion dollars of insurance in force has assets of over 1 billion 375 million dollars.

Rounding out the state's billion-dollar companies are Northern States Power, a utility, and the Carlson Companies, a diversified privately held firm that operates hotels, owns the Gold Bond Stamp Co. and is involved in many other activities.

Although there are no billion-dollar, Minnesota-based companies connected with them, no description of Minnesota business would be complete without including the timber and mining industries. Both had their heydays years ago, yet both remain valuable to the present economy.

More than 56,000 Minnesotans are employed in producing the state's $1.5-billion output of wood products. The state still has nearly 14 million acres of commercial forestland, and, with today's emphasis on reforestation, the industry is certain to remain an important part of the business community.

Mining, too, is still a vital business for northern Minnesota, but the bountiful days of the nearly pure iron ore are gone forever. It's difficult to realize that, between 1895 and 1960, Minnesota produced more than half the iron used in the entire country, about two-and-a-half *billion* tons. There are still billions of tons of the less valuable taconite ore remaining in northern Minnesota and several other valuable minerals as well, so mining will also contribute much in the years ahead.

Most of the industries discussed so far were formed because people needed the products and services they offered, but a few industries began in Minnesota just to take care of the growing needs of business itself. Graphic arts is one. Minnesota ranks among the top five centers in the country in this type of service.

That Minnesota is a highly unusual and active business center is indisputable. The reasons for this are sometimes obscure and frequently complex but always fascinating.

Billion-Dollar Corporations

Population (in millions)	State	Number of Corporations
18.3	New York	123
11.2	Illinois	55
20.0	California	52
10.7	Ohio	41
11.8	Pennsylvania	36
3.1	Connecticut	29
11.2	Texas	27
3.8	**Minnesota**	24
8.9	Michigan	22
7.2	New Jersey	21
4.7	Missouri	14
5.7	Massachusetts	12
6.8	Florida	8
4.6	Georgia	8
5.1	North Carolina	8
3.4	Washington	7
.5	Delaware	6
5.2	Indiana	6
2.1	Oregon	6
4.6	Virginia	6
4.4	Wisconsin	5
2.6	Oklahoma	5
1.8	Arizona	4
3.9	Maryland	4
1.5	Nebraska	3
3.9	Tennessee	3
.7	Idaho	2
2.8	Iowa	2
2.3	Kansas	2
3.6	Louisiana	2
3.4	Alabama	1
1.9	Arkansas	1
2.2	Colorado	1
.8	Hawaii	1
1.0	Rhode Island	1

(Washington, D.C., is the headquarters for three billion-dollar corporations. States not listed have none located there.)

Minnesota's 23 Largest Businesses

Company	Location	Sales (in billions)
Cargill	Minnetonka	$12.6
3M Co.	Maplewood	4.7
Honeywell	Minneapolis	3.6
General Mills	Golden Valley	3.3
Super Valu	Hopkins	3.0
Dayton Hudson	Minneapolis	3.0
Burlington Northern	St. Paul	2.5
Land O'Lakes	Minneapolis	2.0
Control Data	Bloomington	1.9
Pillsbury	Minneapolis	1.7
Gamble Skogmo	St. Louis Park	1.5
Geo. A. Hormel	Austin	1.3
Grain Terminal Ass'n.	Minneapolis	1.3
Northwest Airlines	St. Paul	1.2
Carlson Companies	Plymouth	1.1

Company	Location	Assets (in billions)
First Bank System	Minneapolis	$10.4
Northwest Banco	Minneapolis	10.0
St. Paul Companies	St. Paul	3.5
IDS	Minneapolis	2.6
Northern States Power	Minneapolis	2.4
Twin City Federal	Minneapolis	2.0
Minnesota Mutual	St. Paul	1.6
Northwestern Nat. Life	Minneapolis	1.6
Midwest Federal	Minneapolis	1.5

Chapter 2

A highly successful Minnesota business executive once was asked what he felt were the key ingredients in taking a company from a struggling enterprise to one that is extremely profitable. "Men, motivation, methods and money," he replied alliteratively.

It probably was no accident that he listed men first. A careful review of the beginning years of many Minnesota corporations—including all 12 of the billion-dollar companies—shows that, almost without exception, each nearly failed sometime in its formative stage. And it's not just accidental that in practically all cases the Herculean efforts of one man—usually the founder or key executive—meant the difference between success or failure. Thus, there's good evidence that one of the primary reasons Minnesota has such an abundance of thriving corporations is the exceptional ability and sheer pluck of its early-day entrepreneurs. Among the hundreds of pioneer business leaders in the pages of Minnesota's history, there were, of course, some typical robber barons, but it's remarkable that a large majority seems to have been unusually honest and highly principled. Those traits, coupled with drive and determination, probably account for a large number of the interesting turnabouts in the history of many Minnesota businesses.

No better example of exceptional integrity can be found than that of Francis Atherton Bean Sr., the founder of what is today International Multifoods in Minneapolis. Bean became manager of his father's flour mill at Faribault, Minn., in 1872. The business prospered until 1890, when a combination of discriminatory railroad freight rates and plummeting flour prices caused the firm, Polar Star Milling Co., to collapse. Creditors were owed about $100,000, a fortune in those days, but there wasn't a cent to pay them.

Two years later, at the age of 50, Bean started over. He learned that the Zimmer flour mill at New Prague had closed and was available for lease. An experienced miller, Bean felt he could make a success of the operation, and, although broke, he approached his brother-in-law, J.H. Mallory, a Rice County farmer, about investing in the business. Mallory placed a second mortgage on his

farm and loaned Bean $1,000. The mill eventually became a suc-
cess, but, in 1896, the owner decided to take over the operations
himself. Undaunted, Bean formed his own company, the New
Prague Flour Mill, Inc., and built his own facility. He slowly
guided the business into a prosperous enterprise, even becoming
international in 1908 with the acquisition of Saskatchewan Flour
Mills Ltd. of Moose Jaw, Saskatchewan, Canada.

Just before Christmas in 1911, Bean went on a secretive two-
week mission, starting in Minneapolis. He first entered the offices
of Bemis Brothers Bag Co., where he was well known as a successful New Prague miller. He asked officials there to dig out the
account of Polar Star Milling Co., the firm he had lost 21 years
earlier. At first, the Bemis people were unable to find it. "Go way
back, more than 20 years," Bean instructed them. Finally locating
it, they saw there was a balance due of $900 but also a notation
that the account was closed, because there was no legal way to collect it from the bankrupt company. Bean said he wanted to settle it
anyhow and asked them to figure out the interest, too, based on
six percent a year. Before he left the Bemis office, Bean wrote out
a check for slightly more than $2,000 to settle the legally uncollec-
tible debt.

Bean then visited Van Dusen-Harrington Co., where he went
through the entire process again. Then, he visited another old
creditor and another and another. Before the two weeks were over,
Bean had personally visited every creditor due any part of the
$100,000 which was outstanding when the Polar Star Milling Co.
went defunct. He paid out more than $200,000 to cover both prin-
cipal and interest. At each place, he requested that the payment of
these old bills be kept quiet.

He probably could have pulled off the entire episode without
fanfare if he hadn't tipped off some friends by saying, just before
leaving on a business trip to Moose Jaw, that he might not be back
by Christmas but that, even if he wasn't, he was going to enjoy the
happiest holiday of his life. Puzzled over the comment, his friends
checked into his whereabouts and learned the full story. They
leaked the incident to a newspaper reporter, and on Dec. 21, 1911,
on the front page of the *Minneapolis Journal* the entire story un-
folded. Here are the first two paragraphs of that article:

> Penniless and $100,000 in debt 21 years ago, a north-
> western miller is observing the 1911 Christmas season by
> distributing $200,000 among men who have absolutely no

legal claim against him, but to whom he owed money when the crash came which left him stranded at middle age. The miller is now 71 years old.

The story of F.A. Bean of New Prague, Minn., reads like a business romance with a Dickens Christmas tale ending. It is a story of a man who lost his fortune, only to give $200,000 away because of a sense of business honor. Not a cent of the $200,000 which Mr. Bean has distributed among his former creditors could have been collected and for every cent of the $100,000 which he originally owed he has paid six percent interest for the entire 21 years. And the best part of the story is that Mr. Bean has enjoined secrecy on every man to whom he has paid money, has said that he didn't want the news to get out that he was paying back the money, that he just wanted to think about it himself, that he owed the money no matter what the law was and that no thanks are due him from the people who are sharing the $200,000 distribution.

It's obvious the example set by Bean had wide influence among other businessmen in Minnesota for years to come.

While most of the Minnesota companies that experienced near-fatal financial crises did so in their very early years—usually because capital couldn't be raised quickly enough or in the amounts needed—there was one notable exception. Geo. A. Hormel & Co. came within inches of bankruptcy a full 30 years after the bustling meatpacking firm had been established in Austin, Minn., in 1891. There's little doubt that the company would have folded during those dark days of 1921 had the founder himself, still robust and actively running the show at 61, not made an impassioned plea before a group of Chicago bankers. Their decision on $3 million in outstanding loans meant the difference between immediate collapse or a second chance.

Hormel told the bankers how he quit school at 13 to go to work in a Chicago packinghouse to help support his family, how he later started his own meatpacking operation in Austin and how he guided the young company to maturity only to run into one of the most unexpected developments any firm could have experienced. He pointed out that closing Geo. A. Hormel & Co. at that time would mean throwing 1,000 men out of work and would cost the town of Austin an annual payroll of $1.5 million, resulting, most likely, in ruining the community, so dependent was it on this single company. Hormel then offered to pledge everything he owned—his stock in the company, his home, his insurance, his other investments, everything he possessed—if the bankers would extend the loans. The sincerity of his appeal obviously impressed the bankers, because they agreed that the meatpacking firm could continue to operate, although with some severe restrictions.

How was it possible for a successful, 30-year-old company, with its hard-working founder still in control, to get into such a bind? For one thing, despite George Hormel's diligence and his insistence upon high quality for all his products, the company was beginning to get too fat. World War I generated a great demand for food, especially meat, and it was getting very easy to sell the firm's entire capacity. Things just were becoming too lax. And then there was the main reason: Ransome J. Thomson.

Called Cy by his many friends and admirers, Thomson was the company's assistant controller and was in charge of the firm's general ledger. He handled the transfer of funds among the many banks used by the corporation, which had sales offices throughout the country. A family man, a Sunday school teacher and community leader, Cy Thomson was highly thought of by officials at Hormel and by Austin's leading citizens. His job provided him with a good salary, but Thomson told everyone he also had inherited a large amount of money from a wealthy aunt. Included in this inheritance, he claimed, was a farm, which straddled the Iowa-Minnesota border near LeRoy, Minn. Because of his new wealth, people weren't overly surprised when some amazing things started to happen at Thomson's farm. He spent about $50,000 converting it into a large chicken ranch, including one building with incubators holding 40,000 eggs. There were two acres of floor space for poultry, and 250,000 chicks were hatched and sold each year. Townspeople weren't even surprised when Thomson paid $10,000 for a champion rooster.

George Hormel and his son, Jay, who was the founder's chief assistant, began to wonder about Cy Thomson when the moonlighting chicken farmer added a dance pavilion at his ranch, which he had named Oak Dale Farms. The pavilion could accommodate 1,000 couples, who danced before a 35-piece band. The interior of the pavilion was designed and furnished by the same decorators who did the Chicago Coliseum and the New York Hippodrome. Oak Dale Farms became a big attraction for residents of southern Minnesota and northern Iowa. Thomson continued to pour money into his project, adding a 10-acre children's playground and a 50-bed hotel, which Thomson said cost him

$50,000. He even added a fire station complete with a permanent full-time fire-fighting crew.

George Hormel called in Thomson to ask about all this sideline activity after Cy bought another farm near Blooming Prairie, a few miles from Austin. Thomson assured his boss that the first farm was making so much money he had financed the second with that income. Hormel wondered if farming wasn't taking too much time away from Thomson's main duties, and it was agreed that Cy's cousin would manage the properties, and Cy, himself, would devote more time to the Hormel books. In the meantime, Thomson's reputation as a fancy country gentleman grew. He put out a catalog which boasted the new Blooming Prairie farm had a Holstein cattle herd worth $300,000. Thomson even paid $25,000 for half-interest in a pedigreed bull to make sure the herd would increase in value. (The bull, it was discovered later, was sterile.)

While George Hormel seemed convinced that Thomson's farming operations weren't interfering with his bookkeeping duties, son Jay was becoming more and more suspicious about the source of funds for the ever-expanding Oak Dale Farms. One Saturday in July 1921, Jay Hormel began poking around the books in the accounting department and discovered a $5,000 company check payable to the Farmers & Merchants State Bank in Austin and carrying the notation, "transfer of funds." A further search showed $5,000 had been credited that same day by the bank to Oak Dale Farms. Thomson was embezzling company funds! The amount was unknown, of course, but it soon became evident why cash was getting so scarce at the meatpacking firm.

Working through the night, Jay Hormel and H.H. Corey, another company official, discovered that, during the preceding six months, Thomson had stolen nearly $500,000. By the time the full investigation was completed, the missing amount totaled $1,187,000, taken over a five-year period. When confronted, Thomson readily admitted the theft, but the enormity of his action didn't seem to alarm him. It did, however, alarm company officials. Geo. A. Hormel & Co. was broke. Disclosure of the missing million dollars came just as the company's $3 million in loans started coming due. Had not the senior Hormel established such an unblemished record for honesty and integrity over the previous 30 years, the company would certainly have folded.

How is it possible for an assistant controller to steal more than a million dollars over five years without being caught? Cy Thomson obviously was a brilliant and very careful man. Despite his many sideline activities, he had not taken a single vacation during those five years. When the outside auditors came around every year, Thomson had his books all in order. That's how clever his scheme was. The key to his nefarious operation was the simple fact that Hormel was dealing with more than a dozen banks scattered around the country—wherever the company had a sales office. Money collected from customers in those cities was deposited in a bank there and then transferred to wherever the firm needed money. Thomson was in charge of those transfers. Secondly, Thomson had somehow convinced officials at Farmers & Merchants State Bank in Austin that the Oak Dale Farms were actually owned by the Hormel company. They had no reason to believe a respected official of the firm would lie to them. Periodically, Thomson would issue a check to the Austin bank, marked "transfer of funds," and then instruct the bank to deposit that amount in the Oak Dale Farms account.

When the outside auditors arrived on schedule, Thomson had already covered his tracks by making a deposit into the Hormel account at the Austin bank in the amount of everything he had already stolen. That balanced the ledger. The deposit, of course, was not backed with real funds. It was just another transfer from one bank to another, which always took several days to clear. He just kept issuing transfer checks to cover the amount of his growing thefts. Although the mounting sum in the company's "funds in transit" account should have alerted someone, there was no auditing of it until after the embezzlement was discovered.

Thomson was sentenced to 15 years in prison for the theft. The Hormel company, naturally, took claim to the Oak Dale Farms, but the operations had been so poorly run and were in such heavy debt that a gain of only $69,000 was realized after everything had been liquidated, still leaving more than a million dollars lost.

While it's hard to imagine any corporate disaster worse than having all of a firm's cash stolen by an employee, at least, in the case of Geo. A. Hormel & Co., it was all over within a few weeks after the embezzlement was discovered, and the efforts of one man solved the problem. In the case of the 3M Co., one severe crisis after another for years marked the beginning of its corporate life, and it took the combined efforts of several men to salvage it. If it hadn't been for the unflinching stubbornness of these key men, 3M would have never survived its early years, for the facts indicate the company *shouldn't* have survived. Not only was it formed with a fraction of the capital needed, but the reason for its very establishment was a colossal mistake.

The company was formed by five men, who had no experience in mining, to mine a product, which, as it turned out, didn't even exist. It took a St. Paul financier and two green farm boys to correct this mistake and eventually to make the company one of the world's largest diversified industrial corporations.

The beginning was a nightmare, and, amazingly, it was a dozen years before there was any hope that 3M could make it. The founders—a doctor, a meat-market manager, a lawyer and two railroad workers—had very little money, no mining knowledge and very little reason to set up business as they did in 1902 at Two Harbors, a village along the shores of Lake Superior. The founders thought they had a large deposit of a valuable mineral called corundum, a rare substance which easily could be marketed as an abrasive. It was several years before 3M discovered its "corundum" actually was a low-grade anorthosite, nearly worthless as an abrasive, or as anything else. Meanwhile, the owners ran out of money constantly, and, whenever they could, they paid their workers and their creditors in stock, two shares of which were worth one shot of bar whiskey in any Two Harbors saloon. The beleaguered investors finally sold 60 percent of their firm for less than $25,000. (In 1979, 60 percent of 3M was worth more than $4 billion!)

Although 3M was founded in July 1902, it was March 1904 before the company's first sale was made—one ton of "corundum" for $20. That was also the *last* sale of the worthless mineral in bulk form. The founders decided to change course when they couldn't peddle the mineral by the sack and set up a sandpaper factory at Duluth, where the "corundum" was to be used in a finished product. That didn't work, either, and it wasn't until the company began using more conventional abrasives that sales finally began to trickle in. By 1906, the firm was selling about $2,500 in sandpaper each month, but expenses were running more than $9,000 a month.

Only the tenacious determination of Lucius Pond Ordway, a St. Paul businessman who poured a good share of his own net worth into 3M, permitted the company to go from blunder to blunder without collapsing. It was Ordway, general manager of Crane and Ordway, a plumbing firm, who bought the 60 percent of 3M in May 1905 by paying off the company's $13,000 in debts and giving it another $12,000 in working capital. Personally worth about a million dollars at that time, Ordway felt a small investment in a mining venture would be a worthwhile gamble. Within the next few years, he pumped better than $250,000 into the company without realizing a penny in return. Before he was through writing check after check to bail out the sickly company, Ordway moved the firm to St. Paul where he could watch it more closely.

The hiring of William Lester McKnight, a South Dakota farm boy, as assistant bookkeeper in May 1907 proved to be the beginning of the turnaround for 3M. McKnight's attention to detail, his aggressiveness and his dedication were badly needed. He was helped immensely by Archibald Granville Bush, another farm lad who also wanted to become a bookkeeper. A.G. Bush joined the firm in 1909. McKnight and Bush kept the company together and slowly improved both plant operations and sales until 1914, when another crisis struck and again almost collapsed the firm.

Things had been running fairly smoothly, and sandpaper sales were gradually improving, reaching a peak of about $22,000 a month. Then, without warning, complaints from customers began to flood the struggling company. The "sand" was falling off the sandpaper shortly after a sheet was put to use, despite the fact that by now 3M was using a superior type of imported garnet as the abrasive. There was no apparent reason why the sandpaper all of a sudden proved to be defective. An all-out investigation, however, showed that an oily substance had somehow found its way into the garnet. Oily garnet just won't stick to paper, and there was no question now that 3M's entire supply was saturated with oil.

It was discovered later that, months before, a Spanish tramp steamer, carrying the bulk garnet bound for 3M, had run into a storm, and olive oil, the other cargo on board, had spilled onto the garnet. When the ship arrived, the garnet had dried out, the oil was not detectable by sight, and the accident was kept secret. The olive oil-saturated garnet didn't prove to be bothersome until the customer started to use the sandpaper. Then it was worthless. 3M had 200 tons of this oil-laden garnet, representing most of the company's working capital. There was no insurance to cover such an unusual accident, and attempts to collect damages from the shipping company proved fruitless. After weeks of experimenting, 3M discovered that by spreading a thin layer of garnet over a metal sheet and heating it thoroughly, the oil could be roasted off. The system worked and 200 tons of materials were salvaged.

There were some minor crises after the olive oil incident, but, from 1914 on, it was mostly a story of progress. With the leadership of McKnight and Bush, plus the boom years in the sandpaper business brought on by World War I and the fantastic growth of the automobile industry, 3M's history was marked with one success after another.

Incidentally, the faith of Ordway, McKnight and Bush in 3M paid off handsomely. All three were more or less forced to take stock in the company instead of cash during the hectic years, and because of that, they each ended their careers with 3M as multi-millionaires. McKnight, in fact, accumulated in excess of a half-billion dollars personally before he died in March 1978 at the age of 90, probably the wealthiest man Minnesota has ever produced.

The amazing ability of pioneer businessmen to survive crisis after crisis, failure after failure and still bounce back to succeed marked many of Minnesota's early entrepreneurs. Take the case of Merritt J. Osborn, founder of Economics Laboratory in St. Paul, who saw his first four businesses fail before he even started the firm that finally flourished.

As advertising manager for the Theo. Hamm Brewing Co. in St. Paul, Osborn was doing well as a salaried worker, but he yearned to have a business of his own. In 1910, he met Herbert Bigelow, the owner of thriving Brown & Bigelow, St. Paul manufacturer of advertising specialties. Bigelow wanted to establish a manufacturing plant for motor trucks, a rather novel product in those days of the horse and wagon. Osborn joined the firm as an officer and was in charge of sales, which went well considering that the product was a poorly constructed vehicle powered by a two-cylinder, two-cycle engine. Osborn managed to sell 25 of them before it became obvious the truck wasn't capable of doing the job for which it was intended.

Osborn fell in love with the trucking business, nevertheless, and was able to get the dealership in St. Paul for the White Motor Truck and the White Steamer Touring Car. He later added the dealership for the Willys-Overland car and the Willys-Knight car. World War I ended that business, however, when cars and trucks were no longer available for civilian use. Osborn then got into a farm tractor business but was unable to obtain scarce material because of the war and was forced to give that up. When the war ended, he became the dealer for the Ford Motor Co. in St. Paul, and later expanded it to a distributorship for the entire Northwest. Henry Ford was going through financial troubles himself in those days, however, and his means of raising capital was to load his distributors with so much inventory, that many of them, including Osborn, collapsed.

With four quick failures behind him, Osborn should have been tempted to go back to the comfortable days of working for a salary, but in 1923, at the age of 44, he took his savings of $5,000 and started Economics Laboratory, Inc., with the idea of making and selling a product for cleaning carpets right on the floor. With neither experience in this new field nor adequate capital, Osborn plunged into his risky venture with no thought of possible failure. His first product, Absorbit, was something less than a smashing success, and although it did, indeed, clean carpeting right on the floor and thus eliminate the need for removing the carpet and taking it out for a cleaning, sales proved to be few and far between.

With almost certain failure staring at him, Osborn came up with a second product, and this one was destined to revolutionize the industrial cleaning field. It was a chemical detergent, which he called Soilax, and it was designed to replace soap in mechanical dishwashers. As effective as Soilax proved to be, it still required a strong selling job, and Osborn was spending more time trying to raise funds to continue operating than he was peddling his new product. Often, he would spend weeks without personally going to his office in the old Endicott Building in downtown St. Paul. Instead, he was in other people's offices trying to sell stock in his fledgling company.

The turning point came several months after the business was established, when Osborn found two St. Paul businessmen on the same day who each agreed to invest $5,000 in Economics Laboratory. The money, from Charles Stott of the Stott Briquet Co., and Alex McDonnell of the Weyerhaeuser Co., provided the breathing room Osborn needed in order to search for additional financing. He finally found it when a Minneapolis man, Paul Puffer, not only bought some stock but also introduced Osborn to friends at the Mayo Clinic in Rochester, Minn. Several of them, including Dr. Charles Mayo's son-in-law, Dr. Charles Berkman, bought stock in the company. For Osborn and Economics Laboratory, it was mostly smooth sailing from that point.

The histories of today's giant Minnesota corporations, reveal that it was almost always the lack of money that caused most of them to nearly fail. And, while capital certainly was a problem in the formation of Northwest Airlines, founded in St. Paul in August 1926, it was the horrendous problems with equipment that plagued this pioneer air carrier.

The company got its start because of accidents which caused two predecessors to fail. The first, operating primarily a mail route between the Twin Cities and Chicago, collapsed shortly after it was started in August 1920, when eight planes were lost and four pilots killed in the first nine months. The second attempt, made by famous air pioneer Charles "Pop" Dickinson in June 1926 to reopen the Twin Cities-Chicago route, failed almost from the beginning. On the very first flight, the pilot, Elmer Partridge, was killed and the plane wrecked. The contract to carry the mail from the Twin Cities to Chicago was then awarded to Col. L.H. Brittin, a St. Paul business leader, who had just raised the capital to form Northwest Airways, Inc. Brittin added mail service to several cities in Wisconsin and, in 1927, began carrying passengers, flying them from his company's base at Holman Field in St. Paul to Chicago for $50 one-way.

From its founding to June 24, 1929, Northwest flew more than a million miles, but, in that brief three-year period, its planes recorded 187 emergency landings because of foul weather and 16 others because of either engine trouble or other reasons. Ironically, it was a series of airplane crashes which helped save Northwest from bankruptcy in 1934. Postmaster General James A. Farley, in a Depression-era economy move, had cancelled all existing airmail contracts, giving the business instead to the U.S. Army Air Corps. The move proved to be a disaster. Ill-equipped to handle such a mammoth undertaking, the Army experienced a series of air crashes and fatalities, and in only a short time, Northwest had its mail-carrying contract back.

Like everyone flying aircraft in those early years, Northwest had its equipment problems, but miraculously it registered 11 years without a single passenger fatality. Then, in January 1938, a Northwest Lockheed-14 passenger plane crashed near Bozeman, Mont., killing all aboard. A few weeks later a second Lockheed-14, flown by Northwest, crashed into a canyon wall near Glendale, Calif., killing everyone. Two months later, in July 1938, a third Lockheed-14 crashed on takeoff at Billings, Mont. Fortunately, there were no fatalities in that accident, but confidence in Northwest's fleet of airplanes sank, and the company was in serious trouble. A wise move by Northwest's president, Croil Hunter, to switch to a fleet of the new 21-passenger DC-3s saved the company.

This wasn't the last equipment crisis for Northwest Airlines, however. By 1948, the company had added several Martin 202s to its growing fleet of aircraft. One crashed that year, and then, disastrously, five more went down in the last 10 months of 1950, again shaking confidence in the company. The Martin 202s were quickly taken out of service and Hunter again faced a challenge to restore faith in the shaken airline. In a personal message to all employees, Hunter told them:

> We must remember that our company became an outstanding airline because it was built on sound foundations, and, in the past, it has met and overcome many obstacles. It is important now that you remember your company's history and the manner in which it has grown and developed into one of the world's great domestic and international airline systems. It is my sincere belief that, with the continued help and cooperation of all of us, the year 1951 may well be one of the most successful years in our company's history.

The company responded, and 1951 was, indeed, one of the most successful years in its history.

In retrospect, it was the failure of others that played a key part in the success of Northwest Airlines. First, the unsuccessful attempts of two other companies to carry the mail to Chicago, and then the abortive efforts of the army to take over the route. Similarly, it was someone else's failure that gave George Draper Dayton his start as a retailer in Minneapolis.

Dayton was a banker at Worthington, Minn., until he decided to move to Minneapolis to engage in real estate. He never had any intention of becoming a merchant. In 1893, at the corner of Sixth Street and Nicollet Avenue in downtown Minneapolis, Dayton constructed an eight-story building which he rented to doctors for their offices. Two years later, fire destroyed the Westminster Presbyterian Church at Nicollet Avenue and Seventh Street, and Dayton was one of those interested in buying the site to construct a commercial building. Ironically, the church committee that decided to sell to Dayton included one William Donaldson of the L.S. Donaldson Department Store across the street. Little did he know that the sale would eventually result in the birth of the Dayton Department Store and, ultimately, one of the nation's largest retailers, the Dayton Hudson Co.

Dayton's original intention for the new property at Seventh and Nicollet was to have the six-story structure he was building used chiefly for offices with some retail outlets on the first floor. Two young Minneapolis men, J.B. Mosher and George Loudon, approached Dayton and informed him they wanted to open a dry goods store on the first floor, but they lacked the necessary capital. Dayton agreed to rent them space and also to furnish $50,000 as working capital. Dayton, however, was to be only a silent partner in the store, receiving rent and dividends from any profit.

The store opened in February 1902, but within a few months, Dayton had plowed more than $100,000 into the venture and was entirely dissatisfied with his two operators. Mosher and Loudon were unable to battle the stiff competition from Donaldson's across the street and soon admitted defeat, selling their interest to Dayton. The store at that time was called the Goodfellow Dry Goods Co. As soon as Dayton took personal command of the store, he changed the name to Dayton's, and his son, Draper Dayton, just out of Princeton, joined his father in running the operation. Although inexperienced in retailing, the father-son Dayton team quickly turned the store around, and the business has shown a profit every year since.

Much of the success can be traced directly to the honest and hard work of George Draper Dayton, who, without question, has been one of Minnesota's most outstanding business leaders. Though he was 45 years old when he started the department store, his penchant for hard work was evident early. When he was only 16, George Dayton took a job at a coal and lumber yard at Starkey, N.Y., near his parents' home. He was to be paid $800 a year plus a three percent commission on everything he sold over a certain amount, a commission the owner of the company never expected he'd have to pay. At the end of the year, Dayton had earned $800 in commissions, and had drawn only $100 of his salary, so he had $1,500 coming. The owner, George McMillan, was unable to pay, and he offered to sell the business to Dayton for the amount he was due plus another $2,000. Dayton borrowed the money from his father and, at the age of 17, was the owner of a coal and lumber yard.

In his youthful exuberance, Dayton decided the only way to make the business profitable was to spend long hours at it. He developed a system where he would work all day, all night, all the next day and then sleep the next night. He thought one night's sleep every two days was enough for a strong, healthy young man. After several months of that schedule, however, he collapsed. While Dayton was sick, his father traded the coal and lumber business for a new brick house at Geneva, N.Y. It was this property that gave Dayton his start in Minnesota. He traded it in 1882 for 640 shares of prairie land near Worthington in the southwest corner of the state.

Dayton developed his land into a profitable farm and financial foothold in a state that has gained much by having him as a citizen, for Dayton's loyalty to Minnesota marked him as an outstanding resident. His feeling toward the state showed clearly in an incident back in February 1911, when an organization called the Reiner Mining Co. was attempting to raise money among Minnesota businessmen for a gold-mining venture in another state. Dayton paid for a two-column advertisement in a Minneapolis newspaper which stated:

> MEN OF MINNESOTA. I have no special investment to call your attention to, therefore I have no personal ax to grind. I simply want to say a few words about our own city and state.
>
> This morning I received a long letter telling about a wonderful Gold Mine and the great opportunity that is to be given certain citizens of this city who can get in on a peculiarly favorable basis. The communication is signed by a reputable citizen who undoubtedly believes all he says. All that is said about this particular venture may be absolutely true. I neither know nor care, but this I do know that there is no gold mine or any other form of investment anywhere in this world that is more certain of paying large dividends than many investments that can be found right here in our own state of Minnesota.
>
> Why go to California or Florida, Alaska or Mexico, Canada or Bermuda, when all around us lie acres of virgin soil anxious to produce great harvests of all kinds of crops, with the very best of markets near by?
>
> Why hunt for uncertain mines, or possible oil wells, or doubtful fisheries, or even better safe investments in every other remote neighborhood when here in Minneapolis are manufacturing plants started in a small way, proving their value, that will eagerly use your surplus capital and pay you well for same?
>
> Why not start a corporation right here that will "stand by" our home industries and strengthen many an honest man in an earnest effort to build up our city and state?
>
> No better, safer investments can be found than choice real estate in Minneapolis, or Minnesota, judiciously handled—time will greatly enhance values, besides the

dividends you can get as you go along.

If the men of Minneapolis would get busy in a determined effort to develop the undeveloped resources of our own state, this city would grow in a way that would amaze those who can see nothing except it be somewhere else. I know it has been said I was too optimistic, but my judgment now is, I have not been optimistic enough. The growth of Minneapolis is coming faster than I had anticipated and I regret I did not take on more real estate.

Men—Study the situation from every conceivable angle. Get a vision of the tremendous possibilities of Minnesota. Get a vision of the certain future of Minneapolis—then all of us study how we can help make possible in our day that which is *going to be* some day.

I am only one of you, but I will try to do my part and expect to find genuine pleasure in actively doing so.

Quit sending your money everywhere else. Invest it nearby where you can see how it is handled—yes, where you can add your advice and energy, which may be of greater value even than cash.

Let it be Minneapolis or Minnesota first, last and all the time.

Dayton's message to business leaders resulted in a $100,000 damage suit by the Reiner Mining Co., which said it was forced to abandon attempts to do business in Minnesota because of his remarks. Dayton won the suit, but it cost him $2,500 for attorney fees to defend himself. "I didn't feel unhappy about it," he said. "The fun was worth all it cost."

While George Dayton—and many other Minnesota business leaders—felt it was heresy for men in their state to invest in enterprises beyond their borders, this provincial attitude didn't extend in the opposite direction. It was perfectly acceptable for Minnesota companies to accept investors from out of state and even out of the country. Dayton himself came to Minnesota originally to represent some Eastern investors who saw an opportunity here for their money to grow.

Several Minnesota corporations would have certainly failed had it not been for money from out-of-state backers. The C.A. Pillsbury Co., in fact, was actually owned by an English financial syndicate about 20 years after its founding in 1869 by Charles A.

Pillsbury. Cargill was rescued in its early years by bankers from New York. The railroads headquartered in Minnesota before the turn of the century couldn't have existed without millions of dollars of capital, both from the East and from foreign countries.

In most cases, investments from outsiders in Minnesota business proved exceedingly rewarding. There were notable exceptions, of course. Both Pillsbury and Northern Pacific went broke while controlled by outside money. Northern Pacific, in fact, went bankrupt twice in its early years as a St. Paul-based railroad.

Pillsbury failed in 1907 for a variety of reasons. Both its founder, Charles A. Pillsbury, and his uncle, the former governor of Minnesota, John Sargent Pillsbury, had died, and the leadership they had provided for nearly four decades was sorely missed. Management had begun to get sloppy, and the panic of 1907 was the last straw. The company was placed in receivership with a veteran milling operator, Albert C. Loring, placed in charge. As is often the case, the crisis proved to be a turning point for the company, and 16 years later, on June 27, 1923, Pillsbury was able to buy out its English owners and once again become a Minnesota-controlled company.

Things weren't so fortunate for the poorly managed Northern Pacific Railroad. It went bankrupt during the panic of 1873, was reorganized only to go into receivership again, along with most of the railroads in the country, during the panic of 1893. James J. Hill's Great Northern Railroad was one of the few to survive those dark years, and that was almost entirely as the result of the dynamic leadership of Hill, possibly the most famous of all Minnesota business leaders, past and present. A shrewd and cunning autocrat, Hill was unlike most of the business leaders described in this chapter and will be dealt with in more detail later.

Most of the crises described so far climaxed with either the founder or chief executive being chiefly responsible for putting out the fire and then leading the way to better times. There's at least one case, however, in which the solution to a pending disaster came with the courageous decision of a top man to leave the company in order to prove the seriousness of the situation.

This unusual turn of events involved North Central Airlines, now called Republic Airlines, and the feisty Hal Carr. Carr had been with North Central almost since its founding toward the end of World War II, and, in 1951, was executive vice president and general manager. The young airline had just undergone rapid expansion and profits were hurting because of the growth. Carr strongly believed the company, then called Wisconsin Central, had to continue to spend money to improve service, but he was running into strong opposition from the directors, who were in a cost-cutting mood.

To slow down would be disastrous, Carr argued. In December 1951, when he failed to get backing, he resigned. Without his leadership, the airline began to stumble, and, before 1952 had ended, the company showed a loss of more than $100,000 for the year. Complete turmoil prevailed in 1953. Bank accounts were overdrawn; creditors were yelling to be paid, and just meeting the payroll was beginning to get difficult. The company, based in the Twin Cities and with its name changed to North Central, was threatened with having its insurance cancelled and its fuel supplies cut off by unpaid creditors. In fact, on one flight, the captain of the airplane had to purchase fuel to complete the flight with his own credit card, because the supplier refused to honor North Central's. Several of the airline's DC-3s were impounded for non-payment of landing fees. The troubles Hal Carr had predicted had arrived.

Carr, meanwhile, was working as a management consultant and was lecturing on management engineering at the Graduate School of Business Administration at American University in Washington, D.C. North Central's directors by now were convinced that Carr was correct in his analysis of the company, and they wanted him back. On April 7, 1954, Carr rejoined the company as president and, at the age of 33, became one of the youngest chief executive officers in the industry.

North Central had lost more than $200,000 in the first three months of 1954, but in the next three months, Carr completely reorganized the company with a widespread housecleaning, pacified creditors and slowed down the losing pattern. By July, the company showed a net profit of $62,000 for the month. Carr arranged for refinancing, and, before the year was over, the airline was out of trouble.

The leadership of men like Carr, the work ethic of men like George Draper Dayton, the integrity of men like Francis Atherton Bean, the tenacity of men like Merritt J. Osborn and the sheer brilliance of men like William McKnight have given companies in Minnesota that extra edge to go from near disaster to roaring success.

Chapter 3

It's interesting to speculate on why Minnesota has such a large and lively business community, why there are more giant billion-dollar corporations headquartered here than a population of fewer than four million people can logically justify and why the state has produced such a long list of notable business leaders. Over the years, observers of the state's business scene have come up with some interesting reasons ranging from a superior work force to the harsh but invigorating climate, which, presumably, contributes to the exceptionally high productivity of the men and women who make it possible for businesses to prosper. Others point to the fact that Minnesota is centrally located, making markets throughout the Unites States readily accessible.

All these factors are certainly important, and they undoubtedly have added to the state's unique position, but these very same conditions also exist in North and South Dakota, Minnesota's neighbors to the west. Productivity comparisons show that workers in the Dakotas are at least equal—and, in some cases, superior—to those in Minnesota. And the climate is even more invigorating. Their locations are more central, too. Yet, there are no giant corporations in either state. Iowa and Wisconsin, which also border on Minnesota, and which also have these important factors working for them, have a handful of billion-dollar firms, but lag far behind Minnesota as business centers.

The simple reason Minnesota has more than two dozen of the country's largest firms headquartered here is that they all started in the state as tiny entities, grew, prospered and found no overwhelming reason for making an expensive move elsewhere. So, the situation boils down to the questions of why they started here in the first place. In most instances, they did so because of the trees. Yes, Minnesota's forest industry is the main reason the state has such vigorous business conditions today. It's ironic that this credit should belong to lumbering, that maligned industry condemned for so long by so many for moving into the state a century ago, mercilessly raping the land and then, when the virgin stands of timber were depleted, departing.

There will always be those who won't agree, those who are so preoccupied with denouncing the lumber barons for their pillaging that they fail to see that, in the 70 years it took to practically denude Minnesota of trees, the timber industry created the need for a prodigious transportation system, and the two of them were responsible for creating the many sound financial institutions we have today. Furthermore, the state's enormous flour-milling industry, which, at one time, was the largest in the nation, would not have started in Minnesota if the trees hadn't been cleared from the land so they could be replaced with miles and miles of wheat fields. And it was capital from the lumber kings that helped to finance the flour mills.

It must be remembered that, when the first white settlers moved into Minnesota, more than 70 percent of the state's total land area was covered with trees. Except in the southwestern corner where the Western prairies begin, the state had very little farm land. Fortunately, much of the timber in Minnesota was the commercially valuable white pine, that produced the lumber to build the homes and businesses of not only the cities in this state but throughout the Midwest. The white pine was the tree most sought by pioneer builders. It was strong but light in weight; it was slow to decay; it was easy to cut and handle. In short, it was ideal.

Lumbering wasn't Minnesota's first business activity, of course. Fur traders had been engaged in a thriving industry here for more than a century before the first sawmill was built. Fur trading, however, was an unimportant episode in Minnesota's business history, and it contributed little to the establishment of a permanent center of commerce. The traffic in furs began to decline in Minnesota in the late 1830s. By 1850, when lumbering took over, it was about gone. While the fur traders were a colorful lot, they had few needs beyond their food, the simple merchandise used in barter with the Indians, a canoe and natural waterways. The timber interests, on the other hand, needed a large work force, equipment to convert trees to lumber and capital to finance their burgeoning operations.

Lumbering actually started in Minnesota in 1837, when Henry H. Sibley, who later was to become governor of the state, and two partners contracted with the Chippewa Indians for permission to cut timber along the St. Croix and Snake Rivers. Sibley, a bright young man who came to Minnesota in 1834 from Detroit at the age of 33, was attracted to the area by its fur-trading activities. Unlike most of those engaged in trafficking furs, Sibley was an educated man, the son of a respected Michigan judge who insisted his children receive formal schooling before seeking their fortunes. Although young Henry Sibley, working out of Mendota, made fast personal progress with the American Fur Co., he was quick to realize there was little future in dealing in animal hides. Even Sibley was stunned, though, by the sudden collapse of fur trading. The panic of 1837 proved disastrous to the troubled industry, already crippled by declining European sales.

Sibley, who was later to become far more famous for his political prowess than for his business achievements, was one of the first to see the vast potential in Minnesota's forests. Unlike the elusive beaver and mink, the giant white pine was visible—as far as the eye could see, and in every direction. As everyone knows today, the forests in Minnesota weren't as extensive as the pioneers believed, and the common thought in the middle of the 19th Century that 100 sawmills working a thousand years couldn't deplete them was false. But put yourself in the place of an early-day cruiser, attempting to estimate the amount of timber available. Going north from what is now the Twin Cities toward the Canadian border, the explorer stops every few miles, climbs the highest tree he can find and sees nothing but towering white pine for 50 miles or so in every direction. Is it any wonder the thinking in those days was that the timber supply was inexhaustible?

Although a sawmill had already been built by the soldiers at Fort Snelling for their own use, the first commercial sawmill was constructed in 1839 on the banks of the St. Croix River at a site later to be called Marine, a name chosen by the founders who came to Minnesota from Marine, Ill. A year later, these enterprising lumber merchants formed the Marine Lumber Co., and Minnesota's first important industry was launched. Other sawmills were soon built near Marine at Stillwater, and that area along the St. Croix became a booming industrial center, with its residents anticipating that in years to come it would be a metropolis rivalling Chicago. The Stillwater-Marine area wasn't the only logical site for sawmill operations, though. The convenient water power available at St. Anthony (now Minneapolis) attracted several new operations, and Winona in southeastern Minnesota, even though not in the heart of the white-pine country, had a strategic location on the Mississippi River, and, by 1860, became the state's third major lumber center.

Within a dozen years after Henry Sibley and his partners began cutting timber, Minnesota was producing enough lumber to build all the homes and businesses being constructed in the state and to export an additional vast amount. A state report shows that in 1859, Minnesota exported 33 million board feet of processed lumber and 71 million uncut logs. By 1860, the value of lumber cut in the Stillwater-Marine area mills was estimated at nearly a half-million dollars. At St. Anthony, it was nearly a quarter-of-a-million dollars and at Winona nearly $100,000. As the timber industry grew, these three areas remained the focal points, primarily because of their natural waterways which provided cheap and convenient tranport for trees and lumber. Railroads soon entered the scene, however, and Duluth became another important lumber center.

The fantastic growth of lumbering in Minnesota in the last half of the 19th Century is difficult to comprehend, and, if translated into today's dollars, it is staggering. In 1860, a little more than a decade away from the beginning of tree-cutting, the total value of all lumber produced in the state was still less than a million dollars. The industry mushroomed as it tried to keep up with the insatiable demand and reached a peak in 1905 of two billion board feet of lumber, produced in Minnesota's more than 300 sawmills and representing a value approaching 50 million dollars.

In the early years, much of the lumber was being used in Minnesota, especially to build St. Paul and, then, Minneapolis. In just one year, 1882, the two cities used 300 million board feet of lumber to meet their building needs. But as the amount of lumber being produced rapidly increased, the bulk of Minnesota's trees were used elsewhere. Minnesota lumber built St. Louis, Omaha, Kansas City, Des Moines and Topeka and hundreds of small villages throughout the Midwest. Large shipments—for everything from matches to carriages—even went to the established Eastern part of the country, and much found its way overseas to Europe and South America. And, as the railroads moved westward, Minnesota lumber provided the rail ties, boxcars and tools.

It's not coincidental that Minnesota's greatest spurt in population growth occurred during the years of the burgeoning lumber industry. In addition to the thousands of workers who came to cut trees and to man the sawmills, immigrants flocked to the state as the trees were removed to begin farming the virgin land. With prized farm land selling for about $1.25 an acre, it's not difficult to see the attraction. Workers were also needed to run the new flour mills, to help build the state's growing network of railroads and to fill the thousands of new jobs made available by the businesses being started to serve the needs of the growing population. It was the timber industry, however, that first brought the railroads and cleared the land for immigrants who grew wheat for the flour mills. Thus, much of the credit for the population growth can be traced directly to lumbering. A decade after Minnesota's first sawmill was built, the state's population was still only about

170,000 people, but, by 1870, when lumbering was beginning to flourish, the official census for Minnesota showed the population at 439,000. By 1890 it was 1.3 million, a staggering 200-percent increase in just 20 years.

The men responsible for guiding the tremendous economic success of lumbering in Minnesota came mostly from Maine and Michigan, two states which earlier had been the main sources of wood products for the nation. But it was a man from Rock Island, Ill., who stood out as Minnesota's timber king—Frederick Weyerhaeuser. Born in Germany in 1834, Weyerhaeuser immigrated to Pennsylvania in 1852, and began work in a brewery. Like so many young men in those days, he couldn't resist moving westward, and, within a few years, he was working in a sawmill at Rock Island. Industrious and bright, Weyerhaeuser was soon put in charge of a mill at nearby Coal Valley, Ill., and, when it went bankrupt with so many others in the panic of 1857, Weyerhaeuser bought it. A couple of years later, he and his brother-in-law, F.C.A. Denkman, bought another sawmill in Rock Island, and his soon-to-be empire was begun.

The story of Frederick Weyerhaeuser from 1860 through the remainder of the century is one of tremendous growth through acquisition, both of lumber companies and of vast amounts of timber lands. He bought additional sawmills in Illinois, before moving on to Wisconsin where he added extensively to his holdings and then to Minnesota where he established his worldwide reputation as the greatest lumber producer in North America. At one time or another, he owned and operated sawmills or other facilities in Rock Island, Ill., in a dozen cities in Wisconsin, in Minneapolis, Knife Falls, Winona, Cloquet, Little Falls, and Virginia in Minnesota and at several locations in Iowa. The key to his success was probably his uncanny ability to acquire timber holdings. In 1890, he and his associates purchased the immense land grant of the Northern Pacific Railroad for their foothold in Minnesota. In 1892, he bought additional rights in Northern Minnesota from a private company and then purchased 50 million feet of stumpage from the St. Paul and Duluth Railroad. A year later, he added all of the holdings of the St. Anthony Lumber Co., nearly 75,000 acres in the northern part of the state. By 1893, Weyerhaeuser was headquartered in St. Paul, and he or companies he controlled dominated the important timber industry in Minnesota. His four sons—John Philip, Charles Augustus, Rudolph Michael and Frederick Edward—all joined their father in the lumber empire, and several grandsons later followed.

At the beginning of the 20th Century, the senior Weyerhaeuser was president of 21 separate corporations involved in lumber and was also active in both banking and railroad circles. He could see that the future in lumbering would soon be westward, and, although active in Minnesota up until his death in 1914, he had long before begun to add to his extensive holdings in the West. The Weyerhaeuser interests moved their headquarters to Tacoma, Wash., but the family's influence is still widely felt in Minnesota and many descendents continue to live and work in the state.

Rivaling Weyerhaeuser as one of the state's most powerful timber kings was Thomas Barlow Walker, who came to Minnesota in 1862 at the age of 22. Before his career ended, he was reputed to be the largest individual owner of pineland in the world, with thousands of acres in Minnesota and huge holdings in California.

Arriving from his hometown of Berea, Ohio, Walker spent his early years in Minnesota as a government surveyor. The job gave him first-hand knowledge of exactly where the best timber in the state was located, and he used this information wisely when he later began to accumulate land in 1874. Within a few years, Walker owned thousands of acres of prime timber land in various parts of Minnesota. His exact holdings have never been fully disclosed, but Walker himself admitted that, by 1891, he and his partner, H.C. Akeley owned more than a billion board feet of pine in the state. To acquire timber land, Walker used Indian script, took advantage of railroad land grants, purchased public lands at auction and, in short, seemed willing to use any technique that would put the trees under his control. His methods were criticized at various times, but it should be remembered that, during those hectic years, the laws governing the buying and selling of land were best described as "loose."

In his heydey, Walker owned a half-billion board feet of pine in Becker, Polk, Beltrami, Cass, Hubbard and Itaska counties alone, cutting 50 million feet a year at his mills there, and making a con-servative quarter-of-a-million dollars annually in net profit with practically no taxes to pay. He also owned sawmills in Minneapolis and several other locations and, at one time, controlled the timber operations in the entire Red River Valley. In addition to the thousands of acres of cleared land and millions of board feet of lumber in the state's homes and other buildings, the Walker legacy in Minnesota includes the Walker Art Center in Minneapolis.

While lumbering reached its peak about 1905, and rapidly

decreased in importance to the state, the industry is far from dead. In 1979, there were still 56,000 workers employed in Minnesota's various forest-products businesses. The value of all trees harvested and of the secondary manufacturing of those products was estimated at $1.5 billion in 1977. There are still nearly 80 sawmills in the state, eight major paper mills and more than a thousand small manufacturers who use the raw materials produced by the state's forests. Minnesota still has 13.7 million acres of commercial forest land—about 27 percent of the total land area of the state. The valuable white pine is mostly gone, but in its place are millions of acres of aspen, birch, spruce, fir, elm, ash and cottonwood. The major difference between today's wood products industry and the immense lumbering operations of a century ago, besides size is the philosophy of today's business leaders. Trees are now regarded as a crop. They are replanted as they are cut so future generations can reap the benefits of an important resource.

Prior to the beginning of the lumber industry in Minnesota, and even for a dozen years after, one of the major problems facing early businessmen was the lack of an effective paper-currency system. Those exchanging furs for trade goods or those fortunate to have gold or silver in their possession survived nicely, but business transactions involving any type of paper currency were hazardous.

In the first half of the 19th Century, most commerce in the Minnesota Territory was dominated by the American Fur Co., and it even issued its own paper currency, called "beaver money," which generally was accepted by those doing business with representatives of the influential organization. The American Fur Co. not only monopolized the fur industry, it also dealt in land, sold general merchandise, carried the mail and even operated a thriving fisheries industry on Lake Superior in the 1830s and 1840s. The fish yield has been estimated at between four and five thousand barrels a year during the 1840s.

Money, however, became more and more scarce in Minnesota as the territory began to grow. During the fur-trading days, practically everything, except the furs, and a few minor items such as wild rice, cranberries and ginseng, was imported. Consequently, the balance of trade was running heavily against Minnesota, making the money supply problem even more critical. One of the major sources of money coming into the territory was the annuity payments made to the Indians by the federal government, but those funds stayed in Minnesota only a short time. The Indians, prior to receiving payment, would buy supplies on credit from the fur traders, and when the bills were paid, the fur traders would then pay their creditors in the East, so the flow seemed always to be out of the territory.

The demand for sound currency became so strong in the middle of the century that interest rates between 36 and 60 percent a year were not uncommon. Several private banks were opened for business in St. Paul in the 1850s, some of them by honest businessmen and some by outright crooks. Newspapers of the time told the story of several fraudulent bankers, including one Isaac Young who opened a "bank of issue" and distributed some authentic-looking "Bank of St. Croix" notes which turned out to be worthless. Another banker, Israel Smith, was dealing in fraudulent bills issued on the "Merchants & Mechanics Bank of Iowa," which, as it later was discovered didn't exist.

Even valid bank notes presented serious problems. They were usually issued by Eastern banks and had to be returned to be redeemed. With transportation so slow in those days, it was sometimes six months before a note was cleared. Because of this cumbersome system, the notes were usually heavily discounted by Minnesota banks. It took a smart banker to evaluate the notes, to spot the phonies and to just stay in business. Private banks in the 1850s weren't required to incorporate, and anyone with some money and a lot of courage could become a banker. Many did, but few survived.

The lumber industry's tremendous growth made it obvious that some type of a sound currency system had to be established. Minnesota settlers were clamoring for statehood, and a solution to the money problems appeared to be a necessary prerequisite. Unfortunately, the situation was becoming so complicated there was no simple way out of the mess, which was becoming more entangled with the exuberance and enthusiasm of the settlers in the growing territory. Speculation in land was rampant, and, according to one early historian, "everyone was going crazy." People were borrowing money at exorbitant interest rates, buying land, selling it at a huge profit and, in the belief they were rich, borrowing more, buying more, selling more until the economy was completely out of control.

This condition was not peculiar to Minnesota. The entire nation was enjoying a boom in the early 1850s, but prosperity especially affected pioneer Minnesota businessmen who couldn't seem to expand fast enough to meet the growing needs. Drawing heavily on their credit, they pushed the banks to the extreme, even though the banks could lend every penny they had with no reserves required.

The boom came to an abrupt end with the panic of 1857, and no area suffered more than Minnesota. When several Eastern banks failed, it signalled disaster for most of the 30 banks which had begun business in the territory. Because of their dependence on Eastern financial institutions, the Minnesota banks quickly toppled, and only a handful of the more conservative ones survived. The real estate boom collapsed within a few months. Building lots in St. Paul and Minneapolis that had been selling for several thousand dollars early in 1857 were going later that year for a few hundred—if buyers could be found. The prosperous merchants who couldn't keep their shelves supplied in the early 1850s couldn't pay their debts, and most went bankrupt along with the majority of other businesses. The rampant optimism in Minnesota quickly went sour, but the panic had proved that strict banking controls and a sound currency system were imperative if the territory was to become a state and if commerce was ever to become established again.

Statehood came in 1858, and a state banking act was adopted that same year. The few banks which remained were required to demonstrate some sound business practices. They were empowered to issue notes, but the issues had to be backed by public stocks deposited with the state. Unfortunately, this early attempt to strengthen the banking system was short-lived. In an attempt to revive the bankrupt railroad network in Minnesota, the state authorized $5 million in loans—by issuing bonds—to pay for rail expansion. The bond issue did not sell, however, and only $2.2 million worth were actually disposed of—and at far below face value. Consequently, when the railroads didn't revive, the state ended up owning them.

This fiasco reflected badly on the new state banks, and faith in the new system was seriously weakened. By 1861, with the situation still not corrected, only four banks were operating in the territory, and it wasn't until two years later, when a federal banking system was formed, that the state's serious money problems began to straighten out.

Throughout this entire period of fiscal madness, one man emerged as a rare, conservative banker who managed to survive while nearly all others in Minnesota were paying the price of unsound financial practices. He was Parker Paine, a lanky, good-looking, middle-aged businessman, born in Maine in 1808, who had been a merchant in Alabama before moving to Minnesota in 1853. Shortly after his arrival, Paine opened a private bank in St. Paul and also dealt in hides and furs. The son of a Maine minister,

Paine was honest, shrewd and, unlike most frontier businessmen, exceedingly cautious. His caution paid off during the 1857 hysteria, when his was one of three banks in St. Paul to remain open.

(Of course, banks weren't the only businesses to suffer during the 1857 crash. One historian noted that of the 158 business establishments in St. Paul's first city directory that year, only 12 remained in 1858. In fact, more than half of St. Paul's population left the territory during the panic.)

Paine taught future bankers in Minnesota a valuable lesson in how to conduct a successful financial institution. One who learned much from Paine was James E. Thompson who arrived in Minnesota in 1859 and, later that year, went into partnership with Paine. Thompson's background was similar to Paine's. A New Englander from Vermont, Thompson had also been a successful merchant in the South before heading for the opportunities he hoped existed on the frontier in Minnesota. Their new bank, Thompson, Paine and Co., opened in St. Paul on Nov. 1, 1859. James Thompson's younger brother, Horace, joined the bank in 1861, and later that year the two brothers split with Paine and formed the Bank of Minnesota. Paine continued to operate his own private bank for another 10 years.

The Thompson brothers went on to organize Minnesota's first bank under the new National Banking Act of 1863. James Thompson was president of the First National Bank of St. Paul; brother Horace was cashier, and the two of them personally put up 60 percent of the $250,000 capital. The rest was supplied by three brothers in the logging industry, Thomas A., William M. and Hugh G. Harrison, and by James C. Burbank and Charles Scheffer. Opening for business in the Thompson's new building at 67 East Third St., the bank prospered from the beginning, weathered several severe depressions and is still operating. Neither of the Thompson brothers lived to see the tremendous growth which was to come later. James Thompson died of a heart attack while fishing in 1870, and brother Horace, who took over as president, died in 1880.

A good indication that banking had finally solved its earlier problems, and that a sound currency system was firmly entrenched in Minnesota, came during the panic of 1873; not a single bank in either St. Paul or Minneapolis failed.

The history of early banking days in Minnesota is not complete without relating the clever takeover of the First National Bank of

St. Paul by Empire Builder James J. Hill, the railroad king. After successfully forming the Great Northern Railroad and shrewdly seizing control of the Northern Pacific Railroad, both headquartered at St. Paul, Hill decided he wanted to go into banking before retiring. He had always had the dream of building a vast railroad empire complete with large land holdings, mining interests and a development company—all under the umbrella of a holding company with its own bank. He decided that bank would be the First National, partly because he was already a stockholder and a director, but mainly because the First was the leading bank in the area. Hill didn't want to pay what the majority of the owners of the First thought the bank was worth, however. When they flatly turned down his offer, Hill wasn't discouraged. Instead, he purchased the Second National Bank of St. Paul, which, as the name indicates, was the second institution to get a national charter. It was a prosperous bank, although lacking the reputation of the First.

Hill paid $1,240,000 for all the capital stock of the Second National Bank, but his objective of owning the First had not changed. The First's major accounts were the Great Northern and Northern Pacific railroads, both controlled by Hill. With Hill now owning the Second, he naturally planned to move those vital accounts to his own bank. Faced with the consequences of losing their main business, the stockholders of the First quickly relented and agreed to sell to Hill at his price. Three months after Hill acquired the Second National Bank, he had purchased the First for $3,350,000. He merged the two into a single bank under the name of the First National Bank.

As usual, Hill got what he wanted.

The business boom of the 1850s, led by the important timber industry and quickly followed by flour milling and railroading, spawned not only the banking system in Minnesota, but also the insurance industry. On March 5, 1853, the St. Paul Fire and Marine Insurance Co. was incorporated by an act of the Fourth Territorial Legislature. It was the first fire insurance firm in Minnesota. Today, known as the St. Paul Companies, it is the oldest existing business corporation in the state, and, with more than $3 billion in assets, it is one of the largest insurance companies in the nation.

Back in 1853, though, the 17 founders of St. Paul Fire and Marine were thinking only that a growing community needed a local firm to meet its insurance needs. During its first year of operations, it collected only $380.40 in premiums, and, even three years after it was organized, it had sold only 203 policies. It's benevolent to say that the company was off to a slow start. From the beginning, however, the company insisted on prompt and full payment of all claims, a philosophy from which it has never strayed, despite a few harrowing episodes. Its first fire loss occurred in 1855, and although the law allowed 60 days in which to make payment, St. Paul Fire and Marine waived this privilege and immediately settled the claim.

There wasn't enough business available in frontier Minnesota to allow the company to grow rapidly, so expansion to other states quickly followed its formation. The Great Chicago Fire in October 1871, which burned for three days and destroyed much of the city, proved the first real test for St. Paul Fire and Marine. The disaster put 50 insurance companies, unable to pay the heavy claims, out of business. Another 80 companies paid as little as four cents on the dollar, but, within 60 days, little St. Paul Fire and Marine had paid every claim, 100 cents on the dollar, even though the $140,000 it cost was 165 percent more than total premiums collected by the firm that year.

J.C. Burbank, president of the company at the time, wrote his shareholders, "Every principle of honor and humanity demands that these losses should be adjusted and paid at once." In order to do so, the shareholders were required to pay an assessment. The Chicago fire was a minor crisis compared to the San Francisco earthquake and fire of 1906. At that time and for many years after, the catastrophe represented the largest single insurance loss in the country with more than $164 million in claims. St. Paul Fire and Marine's share was $1,267,000, about equal to the company's total capital at the time. Again, every claim was paid in full, and, as in the Chicago fire, the St. Paul Fire and Marine was one of the few companies able to do so. Other catastrophic losses, panics, depressions, wars and investment crashes followed, but the company weathered them all and today stands as one of the soundest businesses in the country.

St. Paul Fire and Marine Co. also played an important role in the formation of Minnesota's first life insurance company, which later evolved into the present Minnesota Mutual Life, now the nation's 17th-largest life insurance firm. It was in Room 15 of the St. Paul Fire and Marine Co. building on the corner of Jackson and Third streets in downtown St. Paul that eight local businessmen met with Russell R. Dorr of Iowa to discuss forming a company to sell life insurance. The date was Aug. 6, 1880. Charles J. Bigelow, then president of St. Paul Fire and Marine, was elected chairman of the new life insurance assessment company, oddly named Bankers Association of Minnesota. Under an assessment company, members paid dues and could be assessed for any extra funds needed for payment of death claims.

The founding members met once a month after forming the firm to establish procedures for the company to follow, and they each received a salary of $120 a year. Dorr, who had the idea of forming the firm but not the capital, was named secretary. Alonzo G. Alcott was elected president, and John B. Sanborn was named vice president. Dr. Daniel W. Hand was the firm's original medical director, and his first examination, that of the president, Alonzo Alcott, was also his first rejection. Alcott could not pass the physical exam necessary to be eligible for life insurance. Two months later, Alcott died, leaving the young company without a president. Dorr replaced him. By the end of the first year, the firm had written $136,000 of life insurance.

During those first months, all business was conducted out of the one-room office in the St. Paul Fire and Marine building with only three full-time employees: Dorr, a male secretary and a salesman. All policies were laboriously hand-written, and each was signed by Chairman Bigelow. In 1883, the company bought a typewriter, one of the first in the state, but even though it produced a letter as clear and handsome as a document from a printing press, Dorr decided it was too slow a process to be used on anything but the most important correspondence. Dorr was also one of the first in the state to replace delicate dip pens with the newly invented fountain pen.

By 1892, the growing company occupied the entire second floor of the St. Paul Fire and Marine Co. building. It was then known as the Bankers Life Association, which more closely described its activities. In 1889, the company had changed from an assessment organization to a more complex type with fixed premiums for its policy holders. In 1901, the company again changed its name to its present one, Minnesota Mutual Life Insurance Co. of St. Paul, a level premium, legal-reserve company.

Minnesota's third insurance company which today has assets of more than a billion dollars, Northwestern National Life Insurance Co., headquartered in Minneapolis, was also formed before the turn of the century. It was founded on Sept. 15, 1885, only five years after the formation of Minnesota Mutual.

Chapter 4

Of all businessmen throughout the state's history who have called Minnesota their home, the most famous—without a doubt—has been James Jerome Hill. The railroad tycoon was publicly called the Empire Builder by everyone, but many privately labeled him a robber baron. Regardless of his reputation, Hill did more to put Minnesota in the national limelight than perhaps any other individual has ever done. Among his multitude of friends and associates were U.S. presidents, foreign kings and the wealthiest of the wealthy. Hill's business tactics were shrewd and ruthless; his determination almost unequalled. His clever takeover of the First National Bank of St. Paul, related in the previous chapter, was accomplished almost effortlessly when Hill was in his mid-70s and long past his prime. In his younger days, he was a real tiger.

No episode concerning the aggressive and ambitious railroading giant better exemplifies him than the facts behind his outrageous "cornering" of Northern Pacific Railroad Co. stock back in May 1901. Hill, almost single-handedly, came within inches of causing the collapse of the country's intricate stock market system during a period when it was considered to be in robust health. Cornering a company's stock, practically impossible to do these days, was not totally uncommon around the turn of the century, but the magnitude of the Northern Pacific debacle was so sudden and unexpected, it caused the ruination of thousands of investors and nearly the collapse of the entire system. Cornering a stock simply means an individual or group has bought practically all the available shares of a company, making it impossible for anyone who has "shorted" the stock to cover his losses.

The Northern Pacific, headquartered, like its rival railroad, the Great Northern, in St. Paul, was a company beset with problems. It had gone bankrupt during the Panic of 1873 and then struggled out of its financial mess to become one of the nation's most powerful railroads only to collapse once again in 1893, during another of the country's many depressions. Hill, firmly entrenched as the absolute monarch of the Great Northern, had wanted to gain control of the Northern Pacific for years, and the financial disaster of 1893 appeared to be the opportunity he needed. Unlike the well managed Great Northern, the Northern

Pacific had lacked forceful leaders and the type of direction it needed to survive. Although already in a shaky position in 1893, the directors insisted that Northern Pacific needed a route to Chicago and, against good advice, had purchased the Wisconsin Central line, probably the worst of the numerous railroads running west out of Chicago. Northern Pacific paid a fancy price for the company, and the mistake proved to be its downfall. Hill moved in almost immediately and offered a reorganization plan which would have his Great Northern buying the Northern Pacific and then merging the two into a single company.

Hill had been long preparing his takeover. He, more than anyone, knew that Northern Pacific's days were numbered, and he patiently waited for the day his shaky competitor would fail. Hill had been quoted earlier that year, in May 1893, saying, "The country will have a panic starting this September which will last for five years." His timing was slightly off. It started in July, and it was probably far more severe than even Hill had expected. In fact, it is now commonly regarded as the most serious depression of the entire 19th century. Northern Pacific—and 191 other U.S. railroads—went bankrupt.

Hill's plan to take over Northern Pacific almost succeeded, but a disgruntled Great Northern stockholder sued Hill on the grounds that the acquisition violated Minnesota's law which prohibited a railroad from buying a parallel line running through the state. As usual, Hill lost the battle but not the war. The law stated a railroad couldn't buy a competing line, but it didn't prevent an individual from acting, so Hill, with the help of his friend, J. Pierpont Morgan, the wealthy Eastern financier, purchased control of Northern Pacific personally. For $4 million in cash, Hill bought effective control, receiving stock in the company which had been worth $26 million just before the panic. Morgan also was heavily involved, but Hill, without question, was in absolute control of both railroads, the second major step in a very ambitious dream.

Never an extremely wealthy man like his friend J. Pierpont Morgan, who had the world's first billion-dollar corporation, the dictatorial Hill, nevertheless, had as much power and authority as any of the Eastern tycoons. Hill's philosophy was simple: own just as much of a corporation as you need to assume effective control, and no more. He was proud of saying in his later years that he never personally owned more than 10 or 12 percent of any company, but he did "own" enough of the other shareholders to make sure there was no doubt as to who was in charge.

Although Hill never confessed to such a great scheme, there can be little doubt from events which followed the takeover of Northern Pacific that his dream was to control all railroading west of Chicago, and perhaps even throughout the nation. He came exceedingly close. Unfortunately for Hill, another powerful railroad titan, Edward H. Harriman, who headquartered in New York City, had a similar and even more ambitious dream. Harriman, who was 53 during the episode of the Northern Pacific cornering, started his rail career by gaining control of the rich Illinois Central. He later added the Union Pacific and then the Southern Pacific to his empire, giving him a system of stretching from Chicago to the West Coast. He, like Hill, wanted to dominate all railroading in the United States, but Harriman also wanted to take over the European rail system, and he even built a line across Siberia, completing his globe-encircling network with fleets of ships on both the Atlantic and Pacific. With the millions of dollars of Rockefeller's Standard Oil and National City Bank behind him, Harriman was a formidable foe for Hill and Morgan.

Hill knew Harriman had the competitive edge on him in 1901, basically because Hill lacked a strong railroad line into Chicago. Hill planned to correct that with the acquisition of the powerful Chicago, Burlington & Quincy line. Before Hill could move, however, word was out that Harriman, mostly to prevent Hill from grabbing it, was rounding up minority shareholders of the Burlington and offering them $80 a share for enough stock to control the company. While Harriman was busy trying to track down the 1,500 small shareholders who owned an average of slightly less than 100 shares each, Hill, with Morgan's backing, made a quick, backdoor deal. Hill approached the controlling owners of the Burlington and offered $200 a share for all 1,075,772 common shares outstanding. The offer was accepted, and, in April 1901, Hill paid nearly a quarter-of-a-billion dollars for complete ownership of the Burlington line. Morgan, who backed Hill with money for the deal, was involved basically for vindictive purposes. The price paid was enormously over the actual value, and it would have taken a miracle for Morgan ever to realize a profit on the deal, but the satisfaction of whipping Harriman probably was worth it. A dozen years earlier, Harriman had beaten Morgan out of control of the Illinois Central, and the egotistical Morgan was still smarting from the defeat.

Now, it was Harriman's turn to be furious. He and Hill controlled every important railroad in the western half of the country, and, if either was to realize his dream, one of the two had to fail, and each was determined it would be the other. Harriman made the first move. He approached Hill with the request that Harriman be placed on the board of the Burlington, and Hill told him, in effect, to get lost. Harriman replied that Hill had just declared a war to the death. Harriman's next move was a cautious one. He began slowly to buy up stock in Northern Pacific on the open market, with the obvious intent to eventually gain control.

At first, Hill was caught off guard, while Morgan and his associates in New York even played into Harriman's hands. On April 1, 1901, Hill and Morgan together owned about $40 million worth of Northern Pacific stock, which amounted to about 25 percent of the outstanding shares. This was more than ample to control the company, because most of the remainder was spread among thousands of shareholders. Harriman began to buy Northern Pacific stock just after Morgan left the country by ship for an art-buying spree in France. Harriman's deliberate timing was excellent. A Morgan associate, Robert Bacon, was left in charge in New York, and when the price of Northern Pacific stock started to rise because of Harriman's active but secret buying, Bacon couldn't resist trying to become a hero in Morgan's absence. The $40 million in Northern Pacific stock that Hill and Morgan owned had been purchased during the preceding four or five years at an average price of only $16 a share. On April 1, the price went to $96, and Bacon began selling without notifying either Hill or Morgan. Bacon did not know, of course, that the stock was going to Harriman, but within the next few days, he had sold off about 35 percent of the total held by Hill and Morgan, even including some Northern Pacific treasury stock, making a profitable killing but falling right into Harriman's trap.

On Friday, April 26, 1901, Hill was in Seattle inspecting rail property, when he was notified by an associate in St. Paul that 106,500 shares of Northern Pacific, an unusually large amount, had been sold in the New York Stock Exchange that day, Hill immediately guessed what Harriman was up to, but never dreamed, of course, that some of his own stock had been sold.

Racing from Seattle to New York by rail, Hill was well aware, that, if Harriman could buy control of Northern Pacific, he would then own two of the four major railroads in the West—the Northern Pacific and the Union Pacific-Southern Pacific—and would have an equal voice in the Burlington, which was, in effect, jointly controlled by the Great Northern and the Northern Pacific. Hill would be left with just one road, the Great Northern, and he most likely would be pressured into disposing of that to Harriman.

Hill, who was then 63 years old and past the prime of most

businessmen, was itching for a fight. He would beat Harriman no matter what. When he reached New York, still unaware that he and Morgan owned far less of Northern Pacific than he thought, Hill was met by Jacob H. Schiff, a former associate who had become a senior partner of the investment firm of Kuhn, Loeb and was aligned with Harriman. Schiff, still friendly with Hill, told him that Harriman now owned 370,000 shares of Northern Pacific common and 420,000 shares of Northern Pacific preferred, which also carried voting rights, and, consequently owned the majority of votes on any Northern Pacific issue and effective control of the railroad.

Hill and Schiff then went to a meeting with Harriman where Hill was told the battle was over, but that Hill could remain in charge if he would agree to throw out J. Pierpont Morgan. Harriman apparently realized, even though Hill had been on the opposite side, he still was the most knowledgeable railroad man in the country. Harriman, and most others in the industry in those days, were basically financial men. Hill was the only chief executive of a major U.S. railroad who understood railroad construction and operation as well as management and finance. Whether Hill was tempted or not is unknown, but it is a fact that he told Harriman he wouldn't be bribed to ditch his friend Morgan, and the battle was far from over.

Later in the day, while poring over stock transfer records in Morgan's New York office, Hill discovered that much of the stock he and Morgan had in Northern Pacific had been sold off. His uproar was pacified somewhat when he learned that while Harriman had the majority of the preferred stock outstanding, he was 40,000 shares from owning the majority of the common shares. Hill also knew that the entire preferred issue could be retired after Jan. 1, 1902, and that the next annual meeting of the corporation in October 1901 could easily be delayed until after the first of the year when Hill and the present directors could get rid of all the preferred shares before Harriman could vote any of his new stock.

Harriman had been told the preferred stock carried voting rights, but he was not aware that those shares could be retired after the first of the year and would then have no weight in controlling the railroad. He learned of this disturbing fact at about the same time Hill was plotting his next move. It was then Saturday, May 4, and Harriman instructed his agent to buy an additional 40,000 shares of Northern Pacific common stock when the market opened the following Monday. He would then have controlling interest of both the preferred and common shares. But Hill was taking action, too. He wired Morgan in France and told him he wanted authority to buy all available shares of Northern Pacific common regardless of price. Morgan, now aware of the full situation, told Hill to go ahead. At this point, fate took an ugly twist for Harriman. His order for the 40,000 shares was never executed. His agent, before entering the buy order, contacted Jacob Schiff for permission to unleash more of the Rockefeller money for the purchase, and Schiff, unaware of the worthless role the preferred stock would play, said no. He figured Harriman already controlled the company and no further buying was necessary. Schiff made the fatal mistake of not contacting Harriman.

When the market opened on Monday, May 6, Hill bought all the Northern Pacific common available, sending the price of a share to $127.50 before the day ended. He kept it up on Tuesday, and the stock went to $143.25. On Wednesday, Northern Pacific common was trading at a high of $180. On Wall Street in those days, when the price of a stock soared as Northern Pacific was doing, it usually meant someone was out for a financial killing, and, when the stock was run up high enough, whoever was masterminding the plot would sell off at a tremendous profit, and the price would plunge. This invited speculators to get in and "short" the stock, which meant they were betting the stock would eventually go down, and they would receive the difference between the price of the stock at the time they shorted it and the price at the time they actually later bought it to cover the short. This frequently involved a staggering profit. The trouble with the Northern Pacific situation was that neither Hill nor Harriman were after stock-market profits. They wanted the stock in order to control the company, and neither had any intention of selling at any price.

The Wall Street speculators were unaware of the motives of Hill and Harriman, and this ignorance nearly caused the collapse of the entire New York financial community. The reason was that, before the week ended, Hill and Harriman owned every share of Northern Pacific common available, so there was none left for the speculators to buy to cover their short positions. In a short trade, the investors must eventually have actual possession of each share before the transaction can be completed. It appeared that half the investment bankers in New York had been shorting Northern Pacific stock in the hope that in a few days they would all be rich. A total of 78,000 shares had been shorted by the speculators.

On Thursday, May 8, trading in Northern Pacific stock opened at $180 but only a few shares were available, and Hill was getting them all. Before the bell rang at the end of the day there were only three shares left and they each went for $1,000. By the time the speculators realized Northern Pacific common had been cornered and there wasn't a single share available for them to cover their shorts, panic broke out. While Northern Pacific stock was hitting the ceiling, almost every other stock was plunging in price. Practically all small investors on margin accounts, even with first-class stocks, were wiped out when they couldn't meet the many margin calls that were coming in. The pandemonium on the floor of the New York Stock Exchange on Thursday and Friday of that week has never been equalled, even during those dark days of 1929 when it appeared the financial world had collapsed.

And a one-eyed Minnesota railroad man was responsible. Jim Hill sat down to study the results of his furious activity. It's interesting to note that, during the week Northern Pacific stock was breaking all records on the exchange, a representative of a St. Paul newspaper confronted Hill in New York and asked him what was happening. Looking the reporter straight in the eye, Hill replied, "I can't explain the rise in Northern Pacific stock." The truth was that, on Friday, April 10, Hill and Morgan owned 53 percent of all Northern Pacific common stock, while Harriman had 46 percent, the amount he started with at the beginning of the week. There was a one percent which couldn't be located. There wasn't one share to aid the speculators who needed 78,000 to prevent the ruination of most investment banking in the country.

Although it was J. P. Morgan who put up most of the money to capture Northern Pacific, Hill himself invested every penny he personally could turn up. At that time, Hill had a net worth of approximately $20 million, and, on April 10, $13 million of that was in Northern Pacific stock. The remainder of his wealth was tied up in assets not liquid enough to convert to cash.

The battle for control of Northern Pacific was over, but Wall Street was still tottering. Hill and Harriman, realizing they had caused the panic and that only they could bail out the investors, held a day-long meeting in New York and finally agreed to release the 78,000 shares the speculators needed—at $150 a share—so the financial institutions wouldn't topple like a row of dominoes. Morgan later even arranged a syndicate of bankers to make available $20 million to put back into the stock market to help revive it. Much damage already had been done, however, and it was too late to save the $200 million that European investors had quickly pulled out of the market during the panic. A three-year bull market had come quickly to an end, and it would be a long time before the events of that week would be forgotten.

Perhaps Hill, Morgan and Harriman should be given some credit for worrying about the plight of those on Wall Street who would have been destroyed without their help, but the facts indicate that these three powerful men were only concerned with their own welfare. They knew that a collapse of the stock market would hurt them, too, and their action to bail out those in trouble has to be attributed to the personal concerns of Hill, Morgan and Harriman. The deal which the three cooked up included putting Harriman on the board of a new holding company which would operate the Great Northern, the Northern Pacific and Burlington. That was step number three in Hill's dream.

The holding company, called Northern Securities Co., Ltd., was incorporated in New Jersey, and one of the main reasons for forming the corporation, in addition to preventing any future takeover attempts, was to absorb surplus earnings from the three Minnesota-based railroads and to keep any dividends from being taxed by the state of Minnesota. In return for a seat on the holding company's board, Harriman had to convert his holdings of Northern Pacific into Northern Securities stock. Harriman also got his lieutenant, Jacob Schiff, on the board, but the two had little power against the Hill-controlled group. Harriman's grand dream died with the Northern Pacific corner, and his empire started to decline. He died in 1909, and his ownership in the St. Paul railroads was sold by his heirs.

The formation of Northern Securities made it one of the largest corporations in the world, and it increased Hill's growing power, but after a three-year battle, with trust-buster President Theodore Roosevelt leading the fight, the U.S. Supreme Court on a split five-to-four decision ruled the organization was illegal and disbanded it. Ironically, long after his death, Hill's railroads were again merged into one company, the present Burlington Northern, in 1970.

Hill's dream of dominating all railroading in the West ended with the dismantling of the Northern Securities Company, but by then he had played a vital role in the development of Minnesota business for nearly half a century, and there's little doubt that his overwhelming influence on many phases of commerce in the state is still being felt today, not only here but throughout the country. Historian Philip Guedella wrote in 1936 that "America's true history was always the history of transportation, in which the names of railroad presidents are more significant than those of presidents of the United States." And Hill's name is usually mentioned before those of Vanderbilt, Gould, Huntington and Harriman.

James J. Hill was born in Ontario, Canada, in 1838. He left there at the age of 18 for New York City, where he hoped to sign on as a sailor on a ship bound for the Orient. Unable to find a ship, he decided to walk and ride across the country to California where, he was certain, he could achieve his goal, but he never made it past Minnesota. Arriving in St. Paul in mid-July 1856, tired and out of money, Hill had no choice but to stay and find a job. He went to work as a shipping clerk for a steamboat line in the bustling Mississippi River port. In that year, 1,090 steamboats arrived in St. Paul, and there was plenty to keep young Hill occupied. His wanderlust didn't strike again until the Civil War began. Hill wanted to enlist, only to be rejected because he had lost an eye in a childhood accident. His bent for entrepreneurship was obvious from his early days in St. Paul, and by 1866 Hill was not only holding down his job with the steamboat line, he was also in fur trading, coal dealing, warehousing, selling and even lending. He soon became the leading coal dealer in St. Paul.

Hill was in his mid-30s when he entered the railroad business, and it was the financial crash of 1873 that gave him his start. While other businessmen were failing, he not only survived the panic but ended up with part of the bankrupt Northern Pacific Railroad. Through a series of complicated deals, extremely hard work and a determination that few men had, Hill had made his first million dollars by 1879. The depression was ending just about that year, and Hill was one of the few Minnesotans to make a fortune during those hard years.

His first railroad, the St. Paul, Minneapolis and Manitoba, ran between St. Paul and Winnipeg. His dream was to extend it to the West Coast. In 1889, he changed the name to the Great Northern, and by 1893 the line was completed to Seattle, Wash. Hill boasted that he had the best and shortest route to the West, a line with the lowest grades and curvature ratios of any. It was, indeed, a magnificently constructed road, and there's little question that the driving force of Hill's personality was behind every mile of track. Hill's managerial ability, his close attention to detail and his ruthless disregard for anyone who stepped in his way can be credited for the amazing fact that the Great Northern was the only major U.S. railroad never to go bankrupt during those early years when transportation dominated U.S. commerce.

Probably Hill's most valuable trait in his struggles to build an empire was his uncanny ability to cultivate wealthy financiers and to convince them to back him completely and without question, even in some rather preposterous-sounding schemes. In his early years, it was New York banker John S. Kennedy who lined up much of Hill's financing, and Kennedy was still active as a Hill supporter in the later years when J. Pierpont Morgan was the major backer of the Empire Builder. It's interesting that at one time or another, Hill was at odds with nearly everyone associated with him, including even his sons, but never once did his abrasive personality get him into conflict with his financial backers.

A devoted family man most of the time, Hill lived in a mansion at 240 Summit Ave. in St. Paul. His next-door neighbor was Frederick Weyerhaeuser, the timber king, who had a long personal and business relationship with Hill. One of those rare men whose principal motivate was power and not money, Hill probably drove himself more relentlessly than did those who goal was strictly profit. Although never in want financially, Hill did not accumulate a huge fortune in his lifetime, though it seems obvious he could have if that had been his goal. Hill's personal records show that his net worth grew from $7.7 million in 1885 to $9.6 million in 1890, that it was $12 million in 1895, $20 million in 1900, and soared to $32 million the next year following the historic Northern Pacific cornering. Shortly before he died in 1916, Hill was worth more than $50 million, certainly a large fortune, but only a fraction of that accumulated later by William McKnight during his career with the 3M Co. in St. Paul.

Typical of Hill's disregard for money just for money's sake was an episode involving some valuable iron-ore property on northern Minnesota's fabulous Mesabi Range. In 1897, two aging lumbermen, C.H. Davis and A.W. Wright, had logged off the timber on thousands of acres in the middle of the Mesabi Range and wanted to sell the property so they could retire. Hill bought the land for $4 million of his personal funds with the idea of holding it until the property appreciated. The value did go up, of course, but instead of taking his profit, Hill sold the land to a trust set up for the benefit of Great Northern shareholders for the same $4 million that he originally paid. The royalties on that land eventually paid the trust $425 million, all of which could have been Hill's personally. Asked once if it wasn't silly to have an arrangement whereby any profit from the property would go to shareholders but any earlier loss would have been borne by him personally, Hill conceded that it was probably silly, but he insisted there had never been much risk, and "besides, I wanted to give it to the trust."

Hill was 78 when he died from complications of an infected

hemorrhoid on May 29, 1916. At 2 p.m., the day of his funeral on May 31, every train on the various Hill railroads stopped for five minutes to honor the man who was a bigger contributor to Minnesota's business history than any other single individual.

Chapter 5

There can be little doubt that railroad men like James J. Hill were daring opportunists. They were, after all, willing to risk millions of dollars (even if the money generally belonged to other people), and indirectly they were responsible for the success of a great amount of business activity in Minnesota other than transportation.

The best example is the grain industry generally and flour milling specifically, which simply could not have achieved their vast impact on the state's commerce without the assistance of a network of railroads. When settlers first moved into Minnesota and began to farm the land, they raised mostly corn, potatoes, oats and vegetables—crops they needed to sustain themselves. But it was only a short time before the necessity of a cash crop became evident. Wheat, in most cases, became that commodity, primarily because it grew easily in the territory's fertile land and had to be transported only relatively short distances where it could be milled into flour. Also there was at the time a great demand for bread, not only in the United States but throughout the world.

It wasn't until after 1870, however, when the rail industry had established itself in Minnesota that flour milling really began to grow rapidly, and the state emerged as the single most important milling center in the world. The state's first flour mill was erected by the soldiers at Fort Snelling in 1821. It was mostly for their own use and had no practical commercial value. Other small mills were constructed later at various sites in Minnesota, almost always near waterways so that the grain could be shipped in and the flour shipped out. In addition, water power was necessary to operate the mills. Minneapolis, which evolved as the dominant site for the growing industry in later years, didn't become an important location until after the 1860s.

For the 40 years after that first grist mill was established at Fort Snelling, there was increasing emphasis on wheat, both as a crop for Minnesota settlers and as the raw material for the new flour milling industry. But there was no method of shipping the flour out of the territory except by the unreliable river traffic, and growth was slow. By 1860, farmers in the state were growing 2 million bushels of wheat, and there were 85 mills in Minnesota, producing about 255,000 barrels of flour worth about $1.3

million. Approximately two-thirds of the flour was consumed in Minnesota and the remainder shipped east at a profit of about $1 per barrel.

During the next decade, production of wheat and flour started to increase sharply. Farmers in 1870 grew nearly 20 million bushels of wheat and the state's 200 millers, most of them in southern Minnesota, produced $7.5 million bushels of flour, over half of which was exported. By now the railroads were moving most of the wheat to the mills and the flour to cities throughout the country and to ports from which it was exported to countries around the world. The growth of the flour industry in Minnesota from 1870 through the World War I years was nothing short of phenomenal. In the decade just before the turn of the century, farmers were annually producing more than 50 million bushels of wheat. There were more than 500 flour mills in the state producing an ever increasing amount of flour reaching a peak of an astounding 20 million barrels by 1915.

In the beginning years of wheat farming in Minnesota, the fertile land would yield as much as 22 bushels an acre, but this dwindled as the soil was sapped of the ingredients necessary to produce such volumes. By 1880, a good yield was 10 bushels per acre, and farmers began to understand that rotating crops was absolutely necessary. As new crops were planted, and the economy changed, much of Minnesota's farm land gave way to corn, oats, barley, hay, potatoes, sugar beets and soybeans. The decline of wheat growing had no overnight impact on the flour milling industry as North and South Dakota, Nebraska and Montana made up the volume needed to keep the Minnesota mills grinding. By around 1930, flour milling was beginning to lose some of its importance here, mainly because there was increasing use of the Great Lakes rather than the railroads. It cost less to ship wheat to Buffalo, New York, by water and mill it there than to mill it in Minnesota and ship the flour east by rail. However, according to statistics in the annual milling directory published by Milling & Baking News, an authoritative trade publication, as far as wheat flour milling is concerned Minnesota still ranks third, after New York and Kansas, with 12 mills having a total capacity of 87,900 hundredweights. And if durum and rye are included, Minnesota ranks first with 16 mills and 125,600 hundredweights.

Five Twin Cities-based corporations, which had their beginnings in flour milling and the grain trading it fostered, are still in business and are among the largest and most influential companies in the state today. One, Cargill, Inc., is one of the largest privately owned companies in the U.S. and among the world's largest non-governmental grain-trading organization. Cargill, highly diversified now, is still heavily involved in grain, the field in which it started back in 1865. At that time, Will Cargill, one of the founders, was among the first to realize that the state's wheat economy would dominate the area for years to come. His main interest—collecting, storing, marketing and shipping the farmers' grain—was given a big boost in the Panic of 1873 when many elevator owners went into bankruptcy and Cargill bought several of them at bargain prices.

Four years after Cargill was founded, another of today's major Twin Cities flour and grain firms, the Pillsbury Co. also began operations at St. Anthony Falls on the banks of the Mississippi River. Charles A. Pillsbury, recently graduated from an Eastern college and newly married, came to St. Anthony at the urging of his uncle, John S. Pillsbury, one of the young state's influential men.

More cautious men shook their heads when a few months later Charles purchased a one-third interest in the Minneapolis Flouring Mill for $10,000. The contract was signed on June 4, 1869, and this is considered the founding date of the Pillsbury company.

Frank Peavey, who founded the Peavey Co. in Minneapolis in 1885, eventually became a grain elevator operator larger even than Cargill for a period of time. His firm today is engaged primarily in food processing, flour milling, grain storage, marketing and retailing. The other two—General Mills, and International Multifoods—were essentially flour millers in the late 1800s, but today are food processors with a wide variety of other interests, including grain marketing.

As these five corporations enter the 1980s with combined annual sales approaching $20 billion, they represent a tremendously positive force in Minnesota, but there is little reason for any of them still to be headquartered here. All are international companies and do only a small fraction of their business in Minnesota. They are based here, like most of the other two dozen billion-dollar corporations calling Minnesota their home, mainly because they were started here. Each of the five companies had a similar beginning in that they were founded by ambitious entrepreneurs from east of Minnesota who saw in the state a unique opportunity to get rich by buying, storing, processing, selling or transporting wheat.

None had a more interesting start than Cargill which, from its humble beginning, grew rapidly almost from the pure sweat of its founders, William Wallace Cargill and his younger brothers, Sam, Jim and Sylvester. Before Will Cargill died in 1909, the company had built or bought grain elevators and warehouses in more than 100 locations in Minnesota, North and South Dakota, Iowa and Wisconsin. Ironically, shortly after Will's death Cargill tottered on the brink of bankruptcy for several years, mostly due to some questionable business ventures outside the grain industry made by Will's oldest son, William S. Cargill.

During his lifetime, however, practically everything Will Cargill touched (if it involved the grain business) succeeded immensely. Born in 1844 on the East Coast, the son of a Scottish sea captain, Will Cargill got into the grain business naturally. His father, tired of the life at sea, bought a small farm near Janesville, Wis., and Will's teenage years were devoted to planting and harvesting wheat. In 1865, after reaching the age of 21, Will set off on his own, landing his first job in Conover, Iowa, stacking grain in a flathouse alongside the railroad tracks. During his three years there Will saved his money and by the time he moved to Austin, Minn., with his new bride, he and two brothers, Sam and Jim, owned five elevators. They were small, but the wooden buildings represented a start for the enterprising Cargill brothers.

During the next few years, the Cargills, with Will handling the financing and Sam the day-to-day operations, bought or built grain elevators in several Minnesota towns along the route of the Southern Minnesota Railroad. The first was at Albert Lea, then Easton, Delavan, Winnebago, Oakland, Minnesota Lake, Mapleton and Good Thunder. Will Cargill financed the expansion mostly through a banker friend in Milwaukee, Robert Elliott, who apparently had tremendous faith in the Cargill brothers. By 1873, the Cargills owned and operated 10 wheat-buying stations in Minnesota with storage space for 67,000 bushels of grain.

The Panic of 1873, one of the most severe of the century, spelled disaster for many businesses in the country, including grain elevators, but the Cargills, through sound business practices, survived and even capitalized on the plummeting economy. The depression was especially hard on the expanding railroads, and most of the western roads, including Jay Cooke's St. Paul-based Northern Pacific, went into receivership. More than 5,000 businesses in the country failed during the first six months of the panic and another 23,000 went under before the depression ended. Included in the failures were many country elevators. The Cargills, with the help of their banker friend, Robert Elliott, sensed a bargain and within the next few years they bought at distress prices another 18 elevators in Minnesota with a capacity of more than 200,000 bushels.

Among the first to recognize the importance of Minnesota's wheat economy, the Cargills also were first to see the advantage of exporting wheat overseas. Their sale of 80,000 bushels of wheat to a Liverpool, England dealer was described at the time (June 22, 1878) as the "first important direct export of grain from Minnesota."

The Cargill brothers made a very effective team with Will the leader and in charge of planning and arranging the financing. Sam, who was described as being as hard-boiled as Will was gentle, was the operating man who attended to the details of day-to-day operations. Jim was the innovator, and it was at his initiative that Cargill expanded into North and South Dakota. Sylvester joined the team for a short time, but struck out on his own and was not directly associated with his brothers for most of his career.

The Cargill brothers were quite secretive about their operations, and much detail of their early years is missing. It's obvious, however, from the written history that does exist, that they were in many different partnerships with other people during the peak building period, but it was always the Cargills who survived as the partnerships were dissolved for one reason or another.

The Cargills entered the Minneapolis picture in 1884 when they added a 100,000-bushel warehouse. They later established headquarters in the downtown area. Will, himself, settled in LaCrosse, Wis., where he built the town's most impressive mansion, but much of the activity in later years was centered in the Twin Cities.

Jim Cargill started his drive to establish the elevator business in the Dakotas in 1883 and within two years had acquired or built elevators in North Dakota. It was during this period that Jim Cargill is credited with inventing the cribbed-type elevator which contained bins strong enough to store grain in bulk. Grain had formerly been stored in bags, and bulk handling was faster, easier, and thus, more economical for both the farmer and elevator operator. By 1887, Jim Cargill had elevators in 47 separate locations—34 in North Dakota and 13 in South Dakota with a combined capacity of 1.3 million bushels. The enormous effort it took to accomplish this in such a few short years also proved disastrous for Jim Cargill, who suffered a nervous breakdown in 1888, from which he never fully recovered.

Will Cargill and his wife had four children, who were in one way or another involved in the family business. They were William S., the eldest, who was born in 1869; then Edna in 1871, Emma in 1874 and Austen in 1888. It was William S. Cargill who almost caused the collapse of the empire built by his father and his father's brothers. Adored by his father, pampered by his mother and spoiled as the favored child of extremely wealthy parents, William S. Cargill had three strikes against him before he even started his own business career. He was 23 years old before he finally went to work in the Cargill business, and, unlike his father, his first job wasn't stacking grain. In fact, by 1903 William S. was in charge of the entire southern Minnesota grain operations and asking for even more responsibility, which he received in quick order through a series of unexpected events. Will's brother, Sam, who had been the steadying influence behind the Cargill operations from the very start and who tolerated no monkey business from his nephew, or anyone else, died in 1903, and shortly after, the older brother, Jim, who by then was partially recovered from his nervous breakdown, suffered an even more severe collapse and had to retire totally. This left the ambitious William S. with only his loving father to convince that there were fortunes to be made in other areas. With the blessing of father Will, the son set out to build his own empire.

The first grand and costly enterprise was in railroading, an industry which had had an extremely poor history as a money maker for anyone in the area with the notable exception of James J. Hill. Undaunted by the fact that practically every railroad in the area except the Great Northern had gone bankrupt at least once in recent years, William S. became heavily involved in starting the LaCrosse & Southeastern Railroad, which traveled 30 miles between LaCrosse and Viroqua, Wis., but had little promise of becoming a profitable operation. The drain of capital from the Cargill companies into the railroad apparently didn't convince Will to halt the project, although it appears obvious he was worried about it. Whether it had anything to do with the stroke Will Cargill suffered in 1904 never will be known, but the illness which left him partially paralyzed, gave the son even more freedom to operate on his own.

With the unprofitable railroad not fulfilling his dream, William S., who wanted to score big in other than the grain industry which made his father's fortune, set out for an extraordinary adventure in Montana. He helped form the Valier-Montana Land and Water Co., which started a huge irrigation project in that state. The project involved constructing mammoth dams, reservoirs and canals around Valier, Mont., at costs that have never been revealed but obviously were immense. One of the dams, about 35 miles from Valier, was 470 feet long with a holding capacity of 30,000 acre feet of water. Another, just six miles from Valier, was even bigger—600 feet long with a capacity of 112,000 acre feet.

More and more money was required to keep the Montana operations going until it apparently became too much for Will Cargill to take lying in his sick bed at LaCrosse. He traveled to Montana by train in the fall of 1909 to inspect the property and to see just what was causing the huge outflow of money. What he learned has never been fully detailed, but the trip proved too much for the 65-year-old ailing founder of a rapidly declining fortune. He was taken ill on his way home and died on October 17, 1909, shortly after arriving back at LaCrosse.

Peculiarly, Will Cargill left no formal will, so his estate was divided equally among his four children. William S., with his father gone and with only a minority interest in the estate, stayed in Montana another year to try to salvage the business there. But with no new source of funds to keep it going he was forced to abandon it. Not surprisingly, he wasn't invited to participate in the Cargill family business, which by now was in serious trouble. In addition to the ill-fated railroad and irrigation fiascos, the grain business had been neglected in the years since Sam died and Will suffered his stroke. The Cargill company came close to failing.

The company's savior was Will Cargill's son-in-law, John H. MacMillan, who had married Will Cargill's daughter, Edna, while the two families lived across the street from each other in LaCrosse. The son of Duncan D. MacMillan, a wealthy LaCrosse businessman, John MacMillan was the same age as William S. Cargill, but he had a far stricter upbringing. He had gone to work in his father's bank at LaCrosse when he was only 15, and by the age of 19 was working at the Osborne-MacMillan Elevator Co. in Minneapolis, learning the grain business from the bottom up. Before John MacMillan was 21, he and his two brothers, Daniel and William, went into business for themselves in Fort Worth, Texas, trying to establish a network of grain elevators and a large ranching operation. The venture lasted seven years before failing but the MacMillan brothers learned important business lessons in the many mistakes they made.

When Will Cargill died in 1909, John MacMillan, who had

joined the Cargill business immediately after the Texas failure, was the likely successor. With the help of the Cargill creditors, bankers and others, John MacMillan struggled for several years to put the company back on its feet, and by 1917 had paid off all the old debts and had completely reorganized the company, including buying out the 25 percent ownership held by William S. Cargill, who died in 1920 at age 51.

All did not run smoothly from that point on (the Great Depression of 1929 was a rough challenge for the company), but much of the credit for pulling the Cargill operations out of its early trouble, and setting the stage for the giant it later became, goes to the founder's son-in-law.

Because of the Cargill company's early start and its close relationship with the railroad interests, it established a strong foothold in the grain business in Minnesota. But it would be inaccurate to say that its dominance was overwhelming. Cargill's main rival was a gentleman from Eastport, Maine, who deservedly gained the reputation of being the "Grain Elevator King of the World."

Frank Hutchinson Peavey established a network of grain elevators from his headquarters in Minneapolis that in a period of less than a quarter of a century outstripped the Cargill holdings. By the time of his unexpected death at the age of 51 in 1901, Peavey owned nearly 450 elevators with a total capacity of more than 10 million bushels of grain. Even though both Peavey and Cargill were in the same business in the same state, there is little evidence they were serious competitors in those unusual days of the late 1880s. It appears the two grain giants staked out different territories, went their own ways, and seldom bothered each other. In the major cities, Minneapolis and Duluth, they shared the business comfortably without cutthroat tactics.

The main difference in the two companies occurred after the founders of each died. Cargill became one of the world's five largest grain dealers. Peavey has become the largest miller of durum wheat used in pasta products and is one of the largest flour millers in the country today. While it remains a significant factor in the grain industry, Peavey operates more than 200 retail stores throughout the heartland of rural America, serving customers in three categories of "do-it-yourself" specialty retailing: building supplies, fabrics for home sewing and general farm and ranch merchandise. Peavey has also entered the consumer foods area and sold its Canadian elevator operations to Cargill in 1974.

Frank Peavey actually started his business career in Sioux City,

Iowa, in 1867, a serious 18-year-old entrepreneur who already had several seasoning years behind him. The son of a lumber and shipping merchant in Maine, young Peavey became the man of the family at age nine when his father died. Selling newspapers to help his family, Peavey learned the value of hard work at an early age and by the time he was 15, he felt he was ready to move West to seek his fortune. Taking a job with a grain firm in Chicago, Peavey stayed there a few years until a grocer from Sioux City met him and offered him a job as a bookkeeper in Iowa. Within a year, Peavey had saved $2,000 and with the grocer, H.D. Booge, as a partner, he opened a farm implement business, which appeared to be making good headway until fire destroyed his building and put the 19-year-old $1,800 in debt.

It wasn't long before Peavey was back in business and by 1871 his brother, James, joined the company. The company's entrance into the grain business was more accidental than deliberate. In order to build up the implement business, the brothers started taking grain from farmers as payment in lieu of cash. This naturally led to building elevators in which to store the grain, and by 1884 the firm had outgrown Sioux City, moving to Minneapolis where there were better opportunities.

An important contribution of Frank Peavey's to the grain industry was his introduction of the concrete grain elevator. Prior to 1880, all grain storage in the U.S. was in wood structures, and fires were frequent and often devastating. Insurance rates, consequently, were exorbitant.

Peavey discussed the problem with C.F. Haglin, a Minneapolis contractor, and concluded that concrete grain tanks would be as good as wooden structures for containing grain, and would reduce fire hazards to a minimum. The result was the first successful use of the "slipform" technique of concrete construction in which the forms for the new concrete were slipped upward, resting on the earlier portions of the walls as they hardened. Peavey's very first structure built on this method still stands today in suburban Minneapolis, just east of Highway 100 and just south of Highway Seven. It is unused bearing only an advertising message. At the time, the structure was designated "Peavey's Folly" by those in the industry who questioned its feasibility.

After this structure was completed, Frank Peavey and his son-in-law, Frank T. Heffelfinger, and C.F. Haglin visited Rumania and Russia to inspect methods of grain storage in those countries. Concrete grain elevators were in common use in those countries and their theory was confirmed. The concrete Peavey elevator in-Duluth was built on their return making it, at the time, the largest grain elevator in the Western Hemisphere.

From that time on concrete became the standard material for grain elevators. In future years, insurance rates dropped by more than 80 percent as the former tremendous fire hazard was removed.

The 1868 fire at Sioux City, which destroyed Frank Peavey's first business, made him a great believer in insurance protection. It worked for him at least twice in later years, once when fire destroyed his new $3.5 million St. Anthony elevator in Minneapolis, including more than a million bushels of wheat. He was fully covered, and the fire failed to slow his growth, much less present a threat to his business success. And when Frank Peavey died in 1901, it was disclosed that only a year earlier, he had taken out a $1 million "key-man" life insurance policy with the company as beneficiary. Only one $48,000 premium had been paid on the policy. The insurance was a big help in the reorganization of the company after his death. This type of policy, not uncommon today, was practically unheard of in 1901, and at the time it was issued there was only one in the country of a larger amount, and that belonged to the eastern financier, George Vanderbilt.

Peavey was succeeded in running the company by his son, George Wright Peavey, and his two sons-in-law, Frank Totton Heffelfinger and Frederick Brown Wells. George Peavey left the business after a few years, but Heffelfinger and Wells jointly ran the company for more than 50 years after the founder's death.

During those same years that the Cargill and Peavey interests were dominating the buying, storing, selling and shipping of wheat in Minnesota, two other famous families, also originally from the East, were playing similar roles in the important flour milling industry. Cadwallader Washburn, who started the company which eventually became General Mills, and Charles A. Pillsbury, founder of the firm which still carries the family name, were vastly different in personality, but both, in their separate styles, built milling empires which were to become among the largest in the world.

Washburn, a business genius, wasn't interested in the day-to-day operations of his various enterprises. He enjoyed planning, financing, and carefully selecting the men he picked to run his operations. He was as involved in politics as he was in commerce. Washburn came from an extraordinary family in Livermore,

Maine. He was in his late 40s when he decided flour milling offered him the type of challenge he was seeking. Before that, he had established an amazing record as a lawmaker, farmer, teacher, lawyer, soldier and real estate dealer. Later on he was a United States Congressman and governor of Wisconsin. Cadwallader's six brothers each had careers almost as prominent as his. Brother Israel was the governor of Maine. Elihu served as U.S. Secretary of State under President Grant and later was minister plenipotentiary to France. Algernon Sidney became a successful banker who always saw that his brothers were adequately financed. Charles Ames was the editor of the San Francisco Daily and minister to Paraguay under President Lincoln. Samuel took to the sea and became captain of his own vessel. William Drew had a career most similar to Cadwallader and was involved not only in flour milling but lumber companies and railroads.

Charles A. Pillsbury, who like Cadwallader Washburn came from a family of high achievers, was totally unlike his rival in other areas. Pillsbury, when he came to Minnesota in 1869 from his native New Hampshire, joined his uncle, John Sargent Pillsbury (later to be governor of Minnesota) in the hardware business in Minneapolis. Charles saw bigger opportunities in flour milling and he purchased the one-third interest in the Minneapolis Flouring Mill for $10,000. The money came from his uncle and his father, George A. Pillsbury, who was still living in the East. Charles Pillsbury was a taskmaster, taking an active role in the day-to-day operations, often negotiating for a better price from the farmers who brought wheat to his mill and constantly watching every detail of his business.

The famous "Pillsbury's Best" XXXX flour brand was registered in 1872. There's an interesting story behind this trademark. Medieval millers adopted the mark "XXX" to refer to the best grade of flour for bread, although its use had died out long before Pillsbury Flour Mills Company first came into being. However, when Charles A. Pillsbury heard the story he said, "If three X's mean the best, then we'll add another just to show that Pillsbury's Best is really best."

The Washburn and Pillsbury families were instrumental in pioneering several revolutionary changes in the U.S. flour milling industry, refinements of which were adopted by mills throughout the world. The most revolutionary discovery was the process which turned Minnesota-grown spring wheat into a grain more valuable than the soft-kernel winter wheat grown in warmer climates. Washburn gets the credit for developing this process through the help of a French millwright, Edmund La Croix. In the old process, the hard-kernel spring wheat left large specks of bran in the flour, giving it a brownish color, and making it much inferior to the white flour produced from winter wheat. La Croix went to work developing a system which involved sieves being passed through blasts of air which blew the white flour up, because it was lighter, and wisked away the heavier brown bran and other impurities. The final product was a pure, white flour, superior to anything previously milled. Another Washburn employee, George T. Smith perfected the La Croix machine. Later, after a prolonged dispute over patent rights, Smith joined Pillsbury as head miller.

The new machines were soon at work in the Pillsbury mills and eventually the entire milling industry changed over. Improved many times since, the La Croix air system is still being used in the flour milling process.

Unfortunately, the "impurities" that were removed included the glutenous portion of the wheat which is most desireable for giving "strength" to the flour. This led to interest in the Hungarian roller mill process. Charles A. Pillsbury and other competitive milling company representatives made several trips to Europe over a two-year period to study the Hungarian "high-milling" or gradual reduction process. Despite the Hungarians' attempts to keep the method secret, Pillsbury obtained several rollers and brought them back to Minneapolis.

In this early roller mill process, the wheat passed through sets of porcelain rollers, with more flour being released from the bran. However, there was a problem with the porcelain rollers in that unless run at low speeds, over heat, they tended to chip and wear unevenly. Washburn's engineer, William de la Barre came up with the idea of using steel rollers throughout and eliminating the porcelain rollers, thus further improving the roller mill process.

One of the most important advantages of the roller mill process is that it yields more middlings, or granular flour particles, than the millstone. After the middlings have been purified, and further reduced, a high-gluten flour of considerable strength is obtained where the gluten was previously lost to the purification process. In fact this flour was so successful in the marketplace that in 1879 Charles Pillsbury began planning for construction of the six story "A" mill, which would be the largest and most modern flour mill in the world. When the first milling unit was completed in 1881, the "A" mill became a showplace of Minneapolis, costing the then staggering sum of a half million dollars. The mill, which is today a major Minneapolis landmark and the only registered national historic landmark in Minnesota, at that time claimed a capacity of 5,000 barrels daily—as much as Pillsbury's four other mills were producing at the time. On completion of the second milling unit in 1882, the "A" mill boasted a total capacity of 7,200 barrels.

The Washburn and Pillsbury families were also instrumental in developing an improved ventilation system in flour mills that drastically reduced the possibility of disastrous explosions and fires resulting from flour dust excess. Credit for developing the safer ventilation system can be traced back to serious fires and explosions which affected both Washburn and Pillsbury. On May 2, 1878, an explosion was heard and felt all over Minneapolis when the Washburn "A" mill was destroyed, and the fire which followed leveled more than half of the city's milling district. Eighteen men were killed in the disaster. In 1881, a similar explosion and fire destroyed several Pillsbury mills in Minneapolis and killed four workers. Both disasters were caused by fine flour dust which filled the air during the milling process. A stray spark could ignite the dust and the explosion that would follow would be more severe than if the material involved had been dynamite.

The man who helped solve the dust problem was William de la Barre, Washburn's mechanical engineer who had originally come to Minneapolis as agent for the Berhns Millstone exhaust device. He installed the first such device in Minneapolis in the Washburn mill. Later developments made flour mills virtually free of explosion and fire danger.

One of Washburn's primary strengths was the ability to find extremely capable people to run his businesses, while he sat back and planned new ventures. He lured another Maine import, John Crosby, to Minneapolis in 1877, and later took him in as an important partner. The Washburn Crosby Co. was to become the nucleus of a later merger that resulted in the General Mills corporation. Crosby, who was 47 when he joined Washburn, had married into the Washburn family years earlier, but his wife had died of tuberculosis, and when it was learned that he was ready to leave the East, he was a natural choice for the Washburn milling operations. In that same year, Washburn hired William Hood Dunwoody with the sole purpose of sending him to England to attempt to open the door for Minneapolis flour in that country.

The English were not receptive to Dunwoody, who was an experienced miller in Philadelphia before joining Washburn, but to the English was a meddling foreigner. Despite personal visits to the giant flour houses in Liverpool and London, Dunwoody could not get the English to even listen to him. They were skeptical about the Minnesota white flour, suspecting that chalk dust or other ingredients had been added to make it so white. Instead of admitting failure, though, Dunwoody went right to the small English bakers and even to housewives, offering them free flour to test against what they had been using. The bakers found the Minnesota flour produced a bread that was not only superior to what they had been baking, but they could also get several more loaves from each barrek, which added substantially to their profits.

The demand for Minnesota flour in England opened an entire new market. In 1877 there were only a few hundred barrels sold, but the following year Minnesota millers exported more than 100,000 barrels to England, and by 1885 this grew to two million barrels and ten years later to four million barrels. The breakthrough changed the outlook for the entire Minnesota flour industry.

Cadwallader Washburn died in 1882 and John Crosby in 1887, leaving Dunwoody the responsibility of carrying on. Feeling inadequate to manage the Washburn Crosby interests by himself, Dunwoody brought in James Stroud Bell in 1888 to manage the company. Bell, whose grandfather and father were both in the flour milling business, was a veteran himself in the industry back East. At 41, Bell was an ideal choice to continue the growth started by Washburn and Crosby. One of Bell's first moves in reorganizing the company was to fire Cadwallader Washburn's brother, William Drew, who had too many diverse interests to satisfy Bell.

The Pillsbury Company was also growing rapidly during this period. After the disastrous explosion and fire in 1881, more capacity was essential so in 1883 a new Pillsbury "B" mill was started adjacent to the location where Charles had entered the milling business in 1869. It was completed in 1885.

A newspaper article the following year called Pillsbury the greatest milling company in the world "doing $15 million of business annually." As the firm marked the end of its second decade of operation in 1889, it was to begin a new era under foreign control.

It was at about that time the English, who had lost much of their domestic flour market to the upstart Minnesotan, decided to retaliate. In 1889 a syndicate of English financiers decided to buy the entire Minnesota milling industry. It succeeded in gaining control of the Pillsbury operations and the two mills of William Drew Washburn, but Bell resisted. By virtue of the combination of the Pillsbury and W.D. Washburn operations, Washburn became an aggressive competitor to his former associates, who, because of Bell's determination, remained independent. It was C.A. Pillsbury who, as managing director of the English operations, negotiated to purchase the C.C. Washburn mills. Pillsbury was hired to run the mills since the English wanted only to own the mills, not to manage them. The syndicate paid Pillsbury a salary that at the time was the largest amount ever received by an executive in the United States.

The English syndicate owned the C.A. Pillsbury & Co. and its three giant mills, the two mills of William Drew Washburn—the Minneapolis and Northern Elevator Co., and two water power companies in Minneapolis. They called the new company, Pillsbury-Washburn Flour Mills Company Ltd. Under Charles Pillsbury's direction, the new English-owned company grew and prospered, but within 10 years Charles wanted to retire from the heavy burden of running the firm. His brother, Fred, who had joined the company, had died a few years before and their father, George A. Pillsbury, who had left the East and gone to work for the firm, died in 1899. Charles was not in good health, even though only 57, and he decided to go to Egypt to find a better climate.

The departure of the able manager occurred just about the time a New York promoter was attempting to form a huge milling trust. Thomas A. McIntyre, a New York financier, hoped to incorporate in one giant company most of the mills in Minneapolis and Duluth, Buffalo, Syracuse, New York City and Milwaukee. He succeeded in buying the eastern mills and those in Duluth. His United States Flour Milling Co. would be complete with the addition of the Pillsbury holdings. The English owners seemed interested in selling, but Charles' uncle, John S. Pillsbury and John's son, Alfred Fiske Pillsbury, waged a mighty campaign against the move.

Alfred had just graduated from the University of Minnesota. He and his bride rushed to the east coast to take the next ship to London where he urged the British stockholders not to sell.

McIntyre needed the Pillsbury mills to make his trust successful but John S., besides holding his own stock held the estates of his brother George A. and nephew Fred C. as well as the stock of Charles who was in Egypt. This combination convinced the

English not to sell. The Pillsburys won and the McIntyre trust failed.

The Pillsbury family eventually regained ownership from the English syndicate, starting in 1907 when the company was forced into receivership, and climaxing in 1923 when the reorganized firm bought out the last of the English ownership.

Thus, after a third of a century, the Pillsbury milling properties were brought back to American ownership. In the interim, flour production had doubled to 28,000 barrels a day.

Today Pillsbury operates eight flour mills and is the country's largest flour miller with the capacity to produce about 114,000 hundredweights per day or 10 percent of U.S. capacity. It is the nation's largest flour exporter and one of the top five grain originators. In addition, it is a major producer of consumer food products with total sales in the grocery store of about $1 billion. It is also the third largest restaurant company in the world.

While Pillsbury was working under the handicap of foreign ownership, the Washburn Crosby company was growing rapidly as an independent firm. With James Stroud Bell capably running the company, his associate, William Hood Dunwoody, wanted to expand the operations into Montana. He had been urged to do so by none other than the Empire Builder James J. Hill, who had expanded the Great Northern Railroad into the West and needed commodities to move on it. Bell opposed the move, so Dunwoody struck out on his own. After 10 years of losses, the Royal Milling Co. of Great Falls, Montana finally started making a profit, and the company eventually joined the Washburn Crosby operations through the merger into the present General Mills. While Dunwoody was building up the Montana company, Bell was expanding Washburn Crosby into Buffalo, N.Y., Kansas City, Mo. and Louisville, Ky. He also found new markets for the company's flour throughout the United States and in many foreign countries.

Bell was the first miller to see the advantage of advertising flour to the housewives of the nation, although he faced strong opposition, even from his own staff. In 1893, Bell experimented with ads in the Ladies Home Journal for the company's Gold Medal flour, spending $10,000 in a brief campaign. The next year he spent $220,000 on national magazine advertising, and from that point on the company became one of the country's biggest advertisers.

Perhaps one of the company's most successful and innovative

means of reaching the consumer came with the "birth" of Betty Crocker in 1921. She came into this world in no ordinary way. The inspiration of Advertising Manager Sam Gale, her surname was selected in honor of a popular company director, William G. Crocker. Her first name was chosen by virtue of its solid, feminine, warm and friendly sound. Betty Crocker's signature, judged for its distinctiveness was the winning entry in a Washburn Crosby employee contest for women. This composite character was made to be the housewife's best friend, offering her wanted and needed advice as she under took homemaking responsibilities.

Bell died in 1915 and was replaced by a management team already in place, all of them relatives of former Washburn Crosby leaders. John Washburn, a nephew of Cadwallader Washburn, John Crosby II, the son of the original Crosby, and James Ford Bell, the son of James Stroud Bell, assumed command of the growing firm with each serving a stint as president. Washburn immediately after the death of James Stroud Bell, then Crosby, and in 1925, James Ford Bell took over at the age of 45. It was Bell who was instrumental in forming the present General Mills in a complicated merger of several milling companies scattered throughout the country.

While Bell was planning the gigantic consolidation, he was summoned to New York by an urgent telegram from the noted underwriting firm, Blair and Co. Not knowing the details of the urgent call, Bell left without consulting any of his associates, and upon arriving in New York discovered that an unnamed Eastern company wanted to buy the Washburn Crosby company. The unexpected offer caught Bell off guard, but when pressed to give a price for the firm, he grabbed a fancy figure out of the air and said $40 million, an amount far in excess of the actual worth. The Blair and Co. representative said he was authorized to pay that much and a handshake confirmed the deal.

Bell went immediately to the phone and called Crosby, who by then was chairman of the board. "I've sold the company," Bell told Crosby. "You have no authority to do that," Crosby screamed at Bell. "I sold the company for $40 million," Bell replied. "You had the authority," Crosby enthusiastically shot back. The documents for the sale were drawn up, and everything for the final agreement was ready when the deal was called off because of the reluctance of one director of the buying company. It turned out to be a fortunate incident for Minnesota.

A few months later, in June 1928, General Mills was formed

with the merger of the Washburn Crosby company in Minneapolis along with its mills at Buffalo, Kansas City and Louisville, and several other companies, including the Royal Milling Co. of Montana, the Rocky Mountain Elevator Co., also of Great Falls; the Kalispell Flour Mill Co. of Kalispell, Mont., and the Red Star Milling Co. of Wichita, Kansas. Within a few months, the newly formed General Mills added other milling companies in Kansas, Texas and Oklahoma, and in early 1929 the Sperry Flour Co. of California joined the brood.

General Mills then had 27 separate companies operating in 16 state with a total daily capacity of 81,700 barrels of flour, 5,950 tons of commercial feeds, 72,000 pounds of cereal products and an elevator capacity of 36 million bushels.

Headquartered in Minneapolis, General Mills became the largest miller in the world.

There were dozens of other flour milling companies in Minnesota during the industry's heyday between 1870 and 1930, even though Pillsbury and Washburn Crosby dominated the scene. Most have long since vanished from the scene with one notable exception—the company founded by Francis Atherton Bean Sr., which has since evolved into the Minneapolis-based International Multifoods. After his Faribault flour mill failed, Bean moved to New Prague and in 1896 founded the New Prague Flour Mill Co. He expanded gradually, both in the United States and Canada, and the firm's name was changed to International Milling. In 1923 the company moved its headquarters to Minneapolis to facilitate the rapid expansion it was planning. Today it is still involved in flour milling but is now a highly diversified company, especially in the areas of food processing and the restaurant business.

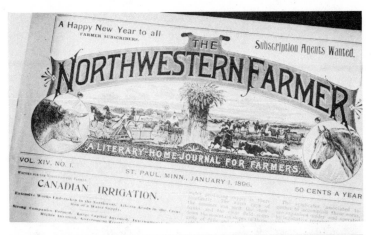

Left, Frank Hutchinson Peavey, the grain elevator king. Top, an 1896 front page of the Northwestern Farmer, the forerunner of the Webb company's famous Farmer magazine. Bottom, the roller equipment used in early Minnesota flour mills.

Top left, Printers Row in early St. Paul. Bottom left, A delivery truck used by International Milling, now International Multifoods, in 1912. Top, James Jerome Hill, St. Paul's famous railroad "Empire Builder."

Top, James Stroud Bell, who rescued Washburn Crosby Co., now General Mills, in 1888. Top right, the first concrete grain elevator in the U.S., called Peavey's Folly in 1889, which is still standing in Minneapolis. Bottom right, Minnesota's famous railroad locomotive, the William Crooks.

Top, Frederick Weyerhaeuser, Minnesota's noted timber tycoon. Top right, Violent street riot during truckers strike in Minnesota in 1934. Bottom right, Wilbur Foshay, right, in jail cell with his attorney after conviction of mail fraud.

Top, Assembly line in early days of Land O'Lakes. Bottom, Land O'Lakes delivery trucks.

Top, Drawing of early Pillsbury flour mill activity. Bottom, Window display for International Milling at store in Moose Jaw, Saskatchewan, Canada, in 1912.

Top, First calendar printing shop at Brown & Bigelow Co. in St. Paul. Bottom, Huge load of cut timber in northern Minnesota. Right, Construction of Foshay Tower, highest skyscraper in Minnesota, completed in 1929 in downtown Minneapolis.

Top, Iron ore docks at Duluth. Bottom, Architect's sketch of Minneapolis home of Washburn Crosby Co. in Flour Exchange Building.

Top, Workman pushes load of flour in early Pillsbury mill. Bottom, One of Super Valu's first Twin Cities grocery stores.

Top, part of three-day ceremony, dedicating new Foshay Tower in downtown Minneapolis in 1929. Bottom, Crew eating breakfast in northern Minnesota lumber camp.

Top, Old stone bridge in Minneapolis, near flour milling center. Bottom, two Peavey Co. ships ready for work.

Chapter 6

The half century between the early 1850s and the first years of the 20th Century firmly established Minnesota as a center for business activity with worldwide implications. Not even the devastating economic panics of 1857, 1873 and 1893—as disruptive as they were—could change the course. Abundant natural resources, forceful leaders and the steady flow of Eastern capital into this area provided an impetus to business that was overwhelming.

First, the seemingly inexhaustible supply of prized timber, then, the valuable wheat crops and the flour milling which followed, assured Minnesota of a railroad network unequalled in the western two-thirds of the country. Even if the northeastern part of the state had contributed no more than an interesting tourist industry, Minnesota was certain to have an important role in the nation's commerce. The fact that the mineral riches located in a relatively small area west of Duluth were to produce a bonanza worth billions of dollars was just frosting on an already delicious cake.

It's a surprising fact to many, even today, that for five decades, starting in the 1890s, Minnesota produced more than half of all the iron used in the entire country—more than 60 percent in the peak years. That represents a staggering amount when you consider the voracious appetite of the automobile industry, the tremendous amounts of steel consumed in two world wars and the generally burgeoning demands of an industrial revolution which completely changed the face of the nation. Approximately two-and-a-half *billion* tons of iron ore have been taken just from the Mesabi range, an area about 100 miles long and not much more than a mile wide.

In retrospect, it appears that the unbelievable wealth created by the rich iron ore in northeastern Minnesota could have had more long-lasting benefits for the state if leaders like James J. Hill, Cadwallader Washburn, Charles Pillsbury, Frank Peavey or George Dayton had been as intensely involved in mining as they were in the fields in which they made their fortunes. Instead, the bulk of the treasure created by the iron ore flowed back East to shrewd capitalists who simply outfoxed the industrious Minnesotans who were long on hard work and dreams but woefully short of the investment dollars it took to develop the mining, and even more lacking in the cunning that business matters required in those days. If J.J. Hill had set his cap for a mining empire instead of a railroad kingdom, Duluth today might be the world headquarters for U.S. Steel. There can be little doubt that iron ore mining has contributed vastly to the economic success of Minnesota, but the big dollars ended up in the hands of such eastern financial geniuses as John D. Rockefeller, J. Pierpont Morgan, Andrew Carnegie, Cyrus McCormick, Marshall Field, Henry Oliver and a host of lesser known capitalists who plainly outsmarted the Minnesotans.

How much iron ore money was siphoned out of Minnesota to the eastern financiers will never be accurately known, but John D. Rockefeller, who never was overly enthusiastic about the prospects of Minnesota mining, realized a net profit of more than $90 million from a relatively small investment in a period of about 10 years. Rockefeller, one of the first to stumble into the opportunity, sold all his mining interests here to U.S. Steel when it was formed in 1901 in exchange for a hefty hunk of the new corporation's stock. Andrew Carnegie, who sold out at the same time, realized an even bigger gain.

Today, there is still a thriving mining industry going on in northeastern Minnesota, but most of the big firms involved are owned by out-of-state corporations. This is in stark contrast to nearly every other industry operating in Minnesota. Back when iron ore was first discovered, however, there was too much euphoria to allow for any concern about the long-lasting effects of this new industry on Minnesota's economy.

The suspicion that there was vast mineral wealth in the Precambrian rocks covering a wide area of northeastern Minnesota had been expressed for many years. Indians native to the area talked about it; fur traders embellished the stories; timber cruisers added fuel to the belief, and early territorial government officials took measures to protect these future riches. Even the U.S. treaty with the Chippewa Indians in 1826, guaranteeing land to the natives, reserved mineral rights in the area to the white man. No one knew for certain what type of minerals existed there, but the hope was, of course, that gold, silver and copper would be predominant.

In the 1840s, before Minnesota became a state, there had been federal surveys by U.S. geologists, who reported that several types of minerals were located in the area just west of Lake Superior. Most references were to iron ore, although no substantial amounts were pinpointed. In the 1850s and 1860s, Gov. Alexander Ramsey,

Gov. Henry Swift and Gov. Stephen Miller all had state geologists surveying wide areas of northeastern Minnesota, hunting primarily for gold, silver and copper. All the surveys mentioned iron ore—one even stating that in the area around Lake Vermilion there was a deposit 60 feet thick—but none of the precious metals was located. Then, in 1865, state geologist Henry H. Eames and his brother, Richard, came back from Lake Vermilion with a find everyone had been hoping for—a rock bearing both gold and silver, which later assayed out to $25 in gold and $5 in silver to the ton. The gold rush of 1865-66 was on.

By early summer of 1866, there were more than 300 prospectors seeking gold in the area, and in anticipation of the eventual discovery, a wagon trail was built from Lake Vermilion to Duluth to carry out the ore. Unfortunately, there wasn't enough gold or silver found to ship even a wagonload of rock, and the mad rush was over before most of the country had even heard of it. Prospectors did find huge amounts of iron ore, nevertheless, and interest in this mineral began to grow. The Panic of 1873 snuffed out attempts to develop further exploration, and it wasn't until the late 1870s that a Duluth businessman, George C. Stone, really became serious about iron ore possibilities. Lacking capital to pursue his interest, Stone, also a Minnesota legislator at the time, contacted a wealthy easterner, Charlemagne Tower, and talked him into financing an iron ore project. Tower, an attorney who represented some iron ore companies in the East, was enthusiastic about new opportunities but leery about investing large amounts of money without some protection. Through Stone's influence in the state legislature, a bill that put a limit of no more than a penny-a-ton tax on any iron ore shipped out of Minnesota was passed in 1881.

Armed with this new law, which assured exceptionally favorable tax treatment for mining interests, Tower financed further exploration in what was to become known as the Vermilion Range. Tower missed the much more valuable Mesabi Range to the south, and it was another decade before this richest area would be tapped by others. Tower, meanwhile, proceeded to form the Minnesota Iron Co. with the help of Stone and another Duluth businessman, George R. Stunz. Together, they bought more than a quarter million dollars' worth of iron-ore-bearing land, and, by 1882, the company had control of 20,000 acres holding more than 40 million tons of iron ore at a total cost of about two cents a ton.

The next step was to build the Duluth and Iron Range Railroad from the town of Tower in the Vermilion ore lands to Two Harbors, getting, in the process, another 500,000 acres in land grants from the state. The first load of iron ore reached Lake Superior via this new railroad in August 1884. Following that first train load of about 200 tons of ore, the Minnesota Iron Co. shipped more than 60,000 tons before the year was over. A quarter-million tons were shipped in 1885 and nearly double that amount two years later. The success of Tower and his new company inspired intensive new exploration, and, by the end of the 1880s, there were nearly 300 iron ore mining companies doing business in the Vermilion range.

It's interesting that Tower, like many of the capitalists who later made it possible for the mining industry to develop here, never set foot in Minnesota, nor even had the slightest curiosity about the state in which he was making a fortune. Perhaps it was the lack of any real roots in Minnesota that caused Tower to give up all his holdings without a fight to the aggressive syndicate controlled by John D. Rockefeller and his brother, William, in 1887. Tower's age (he was 78) certainly was a factor in backing down shortly after his refusal to sell the profitable Duluth and Iron Range Railroad to the Rockefellers. When the Standard Oil millionaires threatened to build their own railroad in Minnesota parallel to Tower's, the fight was over. Tower, who controlled the Minnesota Iron Co., sold its mines and land holdings, plus the railroad, to the Rockefellers for about $6 million and a small interest in the new syndicate. The Rockefellers, who also had iron ore interests in Cuba and Michigan, had made their first, but by far not their last, move into a Minnesota adventure.

All this was happening on the Vermilion Range, but just south of it the Mesabi Range, a sleeping giant, was being awakened. No one knew then how important the Mesabi was to become, but by the time most of the nearly pure iron ore had been removed from Minnesota, the Mesabi had produced in excess of two-thirds of it. Among the first to suspect the potential of the Mesabi wealth was a Duluth timber cruiser, Lewis Howell Merritt. He had taken part in the 1865-66 gold rush and had since then been nagged by the feeling, partly from first-hand observation, that vast amounts of iron ore were waiting for the grabbing south of the Vermilion Range. Merritt passed along this obsession to his eight sons and his five grandsons, several of whom became more infected than he was. Lewis Howell Merritt died before his sons and grandsons discovered the rich deposits on the Mesabi Range, but he never lost faith that the iron ore was there.

Merritt's sons, Lon, Cassius, Alfred, Lewis J., Napoleon, Lucien, Andrus and Jerome, weren't all prospectors, despite the categorization applied to them by most historians. Jerome was a school teacher and Lucien a Methodist preacher. And the famous "Seven Iron Men" referred to when the Merritt family is mentioned included some of the brothers' sons, John E., Wilbur, Bert, Alva and John J. Lon, whose real first name was Leonidas, was the leader of the clan.

By 1890, the Merritts had spent nearly $20,000, all the capital they had, searching in vain for a deposit which was worth mining. Like all prospectors in those days, they were hunting for hard rock, and they had no idea they had been walking on loose soil which contained nearly 65 percent pure iron. The discovery came on Nov. 16, 1890, when J.A. Nichols, who worked for the Merritts, got his wagon stuck in the soft, red-colored soil that covered much of the land in the area they were searching. A closer examination of the dust-like powder prompted the Merritts to have it analyzed, and the results gave renewed life to the Seven Iron Men. The ore, called soft hematite, was the first discovery in the Mesabi and was taken from a site near what is now Mountain Iron. It excited the Merritts, but failed to arouse much interest among the so-called mining experts they later consulted. The soft dirt was scoffed at, not because it wasn't ladened with iron ore, but because the experts agreed it was impossible to economically mine anything but hard rock. "What would hold up the walls of the mine," the Merritts were asked. One geologist told them that flat deposits of iron ore of acceptable purity were unknown in the world and that their discovery on the Mesabi was worthless.

The reluctance of mining people to support the Merritts probably was a break for them in the long run. Instead of starting a stampede by others to the Mesabi, the Merritts had the area pretty much to themselves, and the pessimism of others failed to deter them. Instead of giving up, Lon Merritt took his campaign to the Minnesota Legislature where he lobbied for a bill that would allow land in the Mesabi to be leased. He argued that present laws saved such land for purchase only by the rich who could afford the $5 to $10 per acre the land would bring. He succeeded in his efforts, and because of the new law, the Merritts eventually were able to lease nearly 23,000 acres of land in the Mesabi Range for only 62 cents per acre.

Money was always a problem for the Merritts, and to continue their quest for iron ore they had to sell the timber holdings they owned, as well as most other personal possessions, and they borrowed from anyone who had faith in their dream. In the spring of

1891, they formed the Biwabik Mountain Iron Co. with John E. Merritt, who had just celebrated his 30th birthday, as general manager, reporting to his uncle Lon. There were no assets in the new company except for the leases on the Mesabi land. The brothers attempted to raise capital in Duluth by selling $100 shares in the company for only $10—and on the installment plan at that! But there were no takers. They were able to raise funds from friends, and they managed to convince the people they hired to take $20 of their $40 monthly wages in cash and the other $20 in company stock.

Ironically, the Merritts' first major find of large amounts of ore was not on their leased land, but on a small parcel owned by a Duluth businessman, John McKinley. Unaware of the Merritts' discovery, but highly suspicious, McKinley agreed to let them work his land, but he demanded $60,000 up front and a royalty of 25 cents per ton. The Merritts, before accepting, checked into McKinley's affairs and learned that he was overextended at his bank and needed cash desperately. McKinley settled for $30,000 and no royalties. Again the Merritts had to go to friends to borrow the money. The arrangement with McKinley proved to be a first-class bargain for the Merritts. The original discovery proved to be an ore bed 500 feet by 550 feet and as deep as they could dig—millions of tons of iron ore, some of it 68 percent pure iron. To get the ore out of the grounds was simple, they just scooped it out.

A serious problem arose, however, in how to ship the ore to Lake Superior where it could be taken to the eastern blast furnaces. The Merritts approached the St. Paul and Duluth Railroad and the Northern Pacific, trying to get them to extend their roads to the mine, but without success. While attempting to resolve the transportation crisis, the Merritts discovered other vast ore deposits—this time on their own leased land—and their prospects for obtaining capital improved. With the financial support of Minnesotans who now were beginning to have faith in the Merritts, the brothers and their sons decided to build their own railroad. In a few short months in 1892, they managed to construct tracks from their mines to Lake Superior at a cost which most likely made Empire Builder James J. Hill squirm in envy. The Merritts spent only $500 on the preliminary survey of the road, and only $10,000 per mile to lay the tracks. They were on their way to becoming empire builders themselves.

Their railroad, the Duluth, Missabe and Northern (the Merritts used an alternate spelling of Mesabi), gave the Merritts the vital link they needed between their immensely profitable mines and Lake Superior, where the ore could be shipped to the steel mills in the East. They had everything they needed, except one vital commodity—money of their own. The Merritts were deeply in debt, and the earnings from their properties weren't coming in as fast as the due dates on their outstanding notes. This problem was considerably alleviated later in 1892, when Henry Oliver, a steel magnate from Pittsburgh, approached the Merritts with a tempting proposition. Oliver, who desperately wanted to get established in the promising Minnesota iron ore activity, offered the Merritts $75,000 in cash, which they needed badly, and 65 cents a ton royalty if they would lease to Oliver one of their properties, the Missabe Mountain Mine. Oliver also guaranteed royalties on at least 400,000 tons of ore per year, assuring the Merritts of more than a quarter-of-a-million dollars annually. The Merritts still had other mines to work, were certain to reap big profits from their new railroad and, without a questions, needed a steady cash flow. They accepted Oliver's offer, a deal which gave the Pittsburgh millionaire an entry into the most profitable venture he would ever have.

In retrospect, the timing of Oliver's proposition was tragic for the Merritts, because shortly thereafter an even better offer came along and was flatly turned down. John D. Rockefeller, the founder of Standard Oil and one of the country's wealthiest industrialists, approached the Merritts with a plan to buy all the Merritts' Minnesota holdings—the iron mines, leases and the railroad. Rockefeller was willing to pay $8 million in cash for the entire package, but he was soundly rejected by the confident Merritt clan. Had they accepted, the Merritts could have retired with more money than they could spend in their lifetimes. As it later turned out, Rockefeller, who operated in a league totally unknown to the backwoods Merritts, got control of all their property for nothing, and the Merritts spent their last years practically penniless.

To understand how this travesty could happen, one has to understand the naivete of the Merritts and the ruthless shrewdness of Rockefeller and his lieutenants, who actually concocted the scheme which brought the Merritts to their knees. The Merritts sincerely believed there was enough wealth in the country for everyone, while the Rockefeller team operated on the assumption that there was never enough for even one person. Before the Merritts were to be squeezed out of their king-of-the-hill role in the Mesabi Range, however, other intersting things were to happen.

Andrew Carnegie, the most powerful steel king in the United States, had heard stories about the fabulous iron ore discoveries in Minnesota. He was told by his chief aide, Henry Clay Frick, "They can fill an entire railroad boxcar of the richest iron ore you've ever seen with just five scoops from a steamshovel." Carnegie was impressed. He already had the largest steel operations in the nation, everything from giant blast furnaces to roller mills, but he lacked one ingredient to give him a complete industrial unit—the iron ore from which to make the steel. Probably aware that the Merritts turned down Rockefeller's generous offer, Carnegie instead went to Henry Oliver, who was feverishly operating the Merritts' Missabe Mountain Mine. Oliver needed cash to expand his mining operations, and Carnegie was more than willing to lend him $500,000 for a one-half interest in the Oliver Mining Co. in Minnesota. One more eastern capitalist had invaded the state.

The Merritts, meanwhile, plugged along in their own style, spending money freely, both on their business ventures and in their personal lives. Remembering their hard-luck days when they had to turn to their friends for capital, the Merritts were now generously returning the kindness many times over. They refused to face up to the cruel fact they were simply not sharp enough businessmen to compete against the Eastern giants. They were sober, hardworking men, and they operated their mines and railroad efficiently, but they were sadly lacking in good accounting procedures, had never heard of the word budget and apparently were without the services of a business manager. The beginning of their downfall came when it was obvious they needed more boxcars to carry the ore to Lake Superior, not just a few dozen but several thousand. There no longer was a doubt, they needed to raise a great deal of money to keep the ore moving in the quantities necessary to operate their own mines at full capacity, and to accommodate the ore from the growing number of other Mesabi Range mines.

The Merritts could have turned to Andrew Carnegie, who was tremendously pleased with his entry into Minnesota iron mining and no doubt was in an expansive mood. Carnegie's chief lieutenant, Henry Clay Frick, was quoted in Frick's biography as saying, "I am fully convinced the decision to engage in mining operations in Minnesota was the most advantageous that ever had been, or ever could be, made by the Carnegie company. The story of the way the Carnegie company acquired its great ore mines on Lake Superior is the story of a huge profit made with hardly a dollar of investment." Frick's comment is an understatement. Within a few years after Carnegie invaded Minnesota, the profits of his huge trust soared from $8 million a year to $40 million a year, much of the gain due directly or indirectly to Minnesota iron ore.

For reasons that have never been explained, however, the Merritts apparently never approached Carnegie for money. Instead, they walked into the Rockefeller lair with their eyes wide open, but their brains were in low gear. The first step was an innocent $400,000 loan from Rockefeller with only some harmless bonds on the Duluth, Missabe and northern Railroad as collateral. The Merritts were in clover. They were actually building their own railroad cars, were making plans to extend their railroad from Superior to Duluth, and were loving the reputation they were getting in Minnesota as the Seven Iron Men, the discoverers of the Mesabi Range. They were playing the roles of millionaire industrialists and loving it; some of the brothers even began wearing white shirts. Even the Panic of 1893 meant nothing to the Merritts. It was something that was happening out East, something which didn't really involve Minnesota or the Merritts. And as long as Rockefeller's right-hand man, the Rev. Frederick T. Gates, was seemingly always on the spot with ready cash every time the Merritts needed it, what could possibly go wrong? The Rev. Mr. Gates, after all, even arranged a personal interview between Lon Merritt and John D. Rockefeller himself in New York. The fact that Rockefeller only discussed the weather and never approached the subject of money or business merely meant to Lon that all the details were being left to Preacher Gates.

To fully appreciate the events which followed the meeting between Rockefeller and Lon Merritt, one must know more about the remarkable Rev. Gates. As a former Minnesotan himself, Gates was one of the few Eastern capitalists who actually was on the scene in the state, not only during the eight years he served as the distinguished pastor of the Central Baptist Church in Minneapolis, but during the later years after he had shed his minister's gown in favor of a businessman's vest as the number-one assistant to the powerful John D. Rockefeller. Associating with important men had always come naturally to Freddie Gates. After all, it was Gates who had become one of the closest confidants of Charles A. Pillsbury, the Minneapolis milling tycoon, and, in fact, had tended to Pillsbury's personal business during the man's final days as he was dying from an incurable disease.

Rockefeller first met Gates during the heated negotiations with Baptist church officials which eventually led Rockefeller to underwrite the establishment of the University of Chicago. Rockefeller was tremendously impressed with the former Minneapolis minister, and, in March 1891, he summoned the 38-year-old Gates to New York. In a detailed biography of the Rockefeller family, the authors, Peter Collier and David Horowitz, relate the conversation between John D. Rockefeller and Gates at that first meeting: "I am in trouble, Mr. Gates," Rockefeller began with uncharacteristic directness. "The pressure of these appeals for gifts has become too great for endurance. I haven't the time or strength, with all my heavy business responsibilities, to deal with these demands properly. I am so constituted as to be unable to give away money with any satisfaction until I have made the most careful inquiry as to the worthiness of the cause. These investigations are now taking more of my time and energy than the Standard Oil itself."

Gates gave up the ministry and went to work full-time for Rockefeller, handling all appeals for donations. For the next 20 years, Gates took charge not only of all of Rockefeller's charity work, but also of all of the millionaire's personal business and some of his trickier commercial schemes. The aggressive Gates expanded his domain from a single office next to Rockefeller's to an operation that occupied three full floors at Rockefeller Center in Manhattan and employed a staff of more than 200 people.

Rockefeller's biographers pictured the two men in stark contrast: "One would have to search over wide areas to find two men who were so completely different in temperament. Mr. Gates was a vivid, outspoken, self-revealing personality who brought an immense gusto to his work; Mr. Rockefeller was quiet, cool, taciturn about his thoughts and purposes, almost stoic in his repression. Mr. Gates had an eloquence which could be passionate when he was aroused; Mr. Rockefeller, when he spoke at all, spoke in a slow, measured fashion, lucidly and penetratingly, but without raising his voice and without gestures. Mr. Gates was overwhelming and sometimes overbearing in argument; Mr. Rockefeller was a man of infinite patience who never showed irritation or spoke chidingly about anybody."

There is little wonder Rockefeller needed a man like Gates to look after some of his affairs not related to Standard Oil. When Gates was hired, Rockefeller had 67 major investments, valued at nearly $23 million, in other than oil-related industries, according to his biographers. He had $13,750,000 invested in 16 different railroads, nearly $3 million in nine mining companies, including those on the Vermilion Range in Minnesota, about $2 million in several banking businesses and another $4 million in various miscellaneous fields.

The need for a sharp-eyed personal-business manager was obvious. Gates soon discovered that at least 20 corporations in which Rockefeller was financially involved were in serious trouble. He immediately started a campaign to either gain control of them for Rockefeller, or to get out of them completely. Ultimately, Rockefeller ended up owning 13 of these businesses, and Gates was made president of all of them.

It was with this background that Gates took personal control of Rockefeller's luke-warm desire to get more heavily engaged in Minnesota iron ore activities. With his involvement in the Vermilion Range already producing huge profits, Rockefeller gave the go-ahead for expansion in Minnesota, but he left the details up to Gates, and the sly techniques used to squeeze out the guileless Merritt family were in reality the doing of Freddie Gates, ex-minister, and not Rockefeller, the robber baron.

It was not Gates' style to move in and roughly push out the Merritts with the massive capital he had behind him. He slyly stole the mines and railroad away from the Merritts without them even being aware of it until, suddenly, their assets were zero. All the while they were falling into Gates' trap, the Merritts regarded the former pastor as their one true friend and benefactor. The Merritts knew that out East they were tramping around in a stange jungle full of snarling tigers, but there always was Freddie Gates around to protect them.

Gates' first shrewd move against the Merritts was to introduce them to Charles H. Wetmore, a New York promoter who represented the American Steel Barge Co. Wetmore convinced the Merritts that they should extend the Duluth, Missabe and Northern Railroad to Duluth, where he would provide the barges to ship their ore to the eastern blast furnaces. This was great for Wetmore, but what would the Merritts get out of such an expansion? Wetmore promised to put up $1.6 million if they would extend the road and build ore docks at Duluth and give him a guarantee that his ships could carry all their ore. This was beginning to sound like a highly beneficial proposition to the Merritts. Their railroad had never had an outlet of its own on Lake Superior. It had linked up with the Duluth and Winnipeg Railroad at Stony Brook on the St. Louis River, and the Duluth and Winnipeg carried the ore to Superior. The arrangement had worked well, until the Duluth and Winnipeg ownership balked at building additional cars, causing a serious bottleneck for the Merritts, who, otherwise, had a smooth operation going.

On Feb. 3, 1893, the Merritts signed an agreement with Gates' friend, Charles H. Wetmore and the American Steel Barge Co. It was a complicated arrangement not fully understood by the Merritts, who thought they had the assurance of enough money to expand their operations. Although they were already more than $2 million in debt, the profitable mines and the valuable railroad were worth many times that, and the Merritts weren't a bit concerned about the future. Even when they learned that John D. Rockefeller himself had bought the American Steel Barge Co., the Merritts didn't become suspicious. It only meant that if Wetmore didn't come through with his promises, the millionaire Rockefeller certainly wouldn't let them down. Wetmore came through, however, at least in the early stages, with small amounts of cash to get the railroad and ore docks started, and the jubilant brothers let the contracts for construction. In all their years of scratching the earth for their fortune, never had things appeared rosier for the Merritts than in the spring of 1893. They had money in the bank and traveled in style aboard their own plush private rail car, as handsomely furnished as anything owned by J.J. Hill.

The Merritts laughed at rumors in the East about problems on Wall Street and even the troubles reported by the U.S. Treasury. They were in solid shape. Not only were their own mines producing huge amounts of ore, but enormous new discoveries were being made all over the Mesabi Range, and the Merritts' expanding railroad would carry every ounce of it at nearly $1 a ton. Things started to sour, however, in May of 1893 when Wetmore, for some strange reason, stopped the flow of money to Duluth. The Merritts needed the balance of the $1.6 million dollars Wetmore had promised, and they needed it badly, especially for payrolls and equipment to keep construction going.

Lon Merritt decided in May to go to New York and straighten out the mess. His workmen were demanding their paychecks, and his creditors were beginning to show their ugly side. He had no success obtaining any money from Wetmore, and the tough economic times were affecting everyone in the East. There was always Freddie Gates, though, and when Lon approached him with a worried frown on a face already wrinkled from the years of prospecting in Minnesota, Gates generously came through with enough cash to keep the people back home satisfied, at least for the present. Of course, there were notes and other documents for

Lon to sign, and not really all that much money, considering how much more would be needed in future months. Lon decided he had better stay in New York and watch things closely.

The Panic of 1893 was in full swing, and even Lon Merritt wasn't laughing anymore. He knew what tight money meant, and he was writing this message back home. Yet, he was still confident things would work out. Gates offered him another loan in June to stave off prospects of a riot by the workers, who had received their May paychecks, but weren't about to miss another. When another month rolled by, and the same cash squeeze occurred again, Lon Merritt once more went back to the friendly Gates to bail him out.

This time Gates had a proposition for a permanent solution, one which appeared to Lon to be most generous, especially since the Merritts didn't have to give up ownership of anything, and it meant a badly needed $500,000 for them immediately. Gates' proposition was this: The Merritts would put their five iron ore mines, the railroad and the ore docks into a new company, to be called the Lake Superior Consolidated Iron Mines Co., which would be incorporated under the liberal New Jersey laws. Gates, then, would get Rockefeller to put in his six mining companies in Cuba and Michigan, although worth only a fraction of the Minnesota properties, would advance the half-million cash and would agree to ship all the ore the new company would produce aboard his fleet of Great Lakes ships. The Merritts would get all the stock in the Lake Superior Consolidated Iron Mines Co., would have the majority of the directors on the new board, and would continue to operate the Minnesota properties. It sounded like a great deal for the Merritts. All Rockefeller wanted was some bonds. Of course, they were first mortgage bonds on all the holdings of the new multi-million-dollar company, but that was just simply protection for Rockefeller in case anything went wrong.

It was the depression year of 1893, however, and, as soon as the deal was signed, everything went wrong. The Merritts tried to sell some stock in their new company to pay off the mountain of debt which was rapidly accumulating, but during a panic nobody is interested in buying stock, they discovered. It was a strange situation for them. Here they were, owners of $20 million in stock of a new company which had tremendous potential, and they couldn't peddle a dime's worth of it. Finally, in desperation, they offered to sell Rockefeller all 90,000 shares at the bargain rate of only $10 a share, with an option to buy back 55,000 shares within a year. Before 1894 was over, the Merritts had spent the $900,000, couldn't buy back the stock, and the option expired. What it meant was that Rockefeller, thanks to Gates' shrewd maneuvering, had become full owner of the Minnesota mining properties, the railroad and the ore docks, worth a conservative $330 million, according to estimates which later came out, and the Merritts were penniless.

Years later, Lon Merritt was to write: "The things that happened at that time are not clear to me. The idea of going down there [to New York City] and losing all this money, not only my money, but my brothers' money, leaving their families stripped, so that they did not even have money to pay streetcar fares, struck me down physically, and, I am sorry to say, for a while mentally."

The Merritts did sue Rockefeller in 1895 for fraud and misrepresentation and were awarded a verdict of nearly a million dollars in damages by the U.S. Circuit Court at Duluth, but the decision was appealed by Rockefeller, the verdict reversed and the case sent back for retrial. The Merritts didn't have the money for another costly trial, and gave up. Two years later, they agreed to sign a document retracting their charge of fraud, and, in return, Rockefeller paid them $500,000, which they used to pay their remaining personal debts. The simple document stated: "It is hereby declared that from recent independent investigations made by us or under our direction, we have become satisfied that no misrepresentation was made nor fraud committed by Mr. Rockefeller, or by his agents or attorneys for him." Lon later reported that he signed the document only "to relieve my family from their destitution and absolute poverty." Gates replied, "We knew, of course, that it might be charged that the retraction had been purchased with the price of the settlement, but we reflected that honest men making true charges of fraud are not accustomed to retract those charges for a price in money put into their hands."

Broken financially, but not in spirit, the Merritts lived out their remaining years in Minnesota, even doing some more prospecting for new beds of ore, but nothing of substance was discovered. When Lon, the leader of the Merritts, died in his 80s on May 9, 1926, his entire estate consisted of $1,500 worth of household goods, $800 in miscellaneous personal possessions and $150 in cash. The Merritts' original property by that time was worth billions of dollars.

Both Rockefeller and Andrew Carnegie had had their fun—and profits—by the first year of the 20th Century. They were ready to retire from business and give their full attention to giving away the fortunes they had amassed during the last half of the previous century. No one *knows* who conceived the original idea for a giant steel trust to control most major iron ore mining and steel manufacturing in the country, but it is generally conceded that everyone *believed* there was only one man who could put together such a combination without wrecking the industry in doing so. That man was J. Pierpont Morgan, the same tycoon who helped that famous Minnesotan, J.J. Hill, corner the market in Northern Pacific stock.

Morgan, with his millions in capital and his egotistical desire to be the biggest financier of all times, clearly felt up to the task. By 1901, through plots and counterplots, he was able to get both Carnegie and Rockefeller to combine all their Minnesota properties—the iron mines, the railroads, the ore docks, and the Great Lakes ore carriers—and their steel plants in the East into one gigantic corporation. United States Steel Co. was the largest trust ever created. The formation of United States Steel, capitalized at an inflated value of $1.4 billion, made everyone involved extremely wealthy. With Carnegie and Rockefeller agreeing to the terms of the trust, it wasn't difficult to convince everyone else, including Henry Oliver, whose Minnesota properties were booming, to join. The one holdout, James J. Hill owned 39,000 acres of Mesabi Range land, and he refused to enter the trust. Instead, he turned over his iron ore properties to the stockholders of his Great Northern Railroad, and they later reached an agreement with United States Steel for it to explore the land and ship out the ore with a guarantee of about $8 million a year, a shrewd proposition for the Hill group. Even without Hill in the original consolidation, the new United States Steel Co. had a firm hold on the iron-and-steel industry, and its main purpose, to allow Carnegie and Rockefeller to retire, was fulfilled. Carnegie received more than $300 million for his Minnesota holdings and his eastern steel plants. Rockefeller received $80 million for his Minnesota mines and railroad and another $9 million for his ore carriers.

Formation of United States Steel was the crowning achievement, also, for the ex-Minnesota minister, Freddie Gates. When he came for Rockefeller's signature on the final papers which made the oil magnate the largest shareholder in United States Steel (Carnegie took his money in bonds), the stoic industrialist said, "Thank you, Mr. Gates, thank you." Gates stared at his boss, and replied curtly, "This time a thank you is not enough." Just how much Gates received for putting together the Rockefeller part of U.S. Steel has never been disclosed, but he always called Rockefeller "a very generous employer."

Within a few years after its formation in 1901, United States Steel ran into temporary financial problems, and the inflated value of the firm was quickly reduced to even less than its real value, but the company managed to survive, largely because of the exceptional profitability of the Minnesota iron ore holdings. Rockefeller, in fact, stated in an interview a few years after United States Steel regained its strength, that if it hadn't been for the Minnesota iron ore properties, "The United States Steel Corporation could not have survived the stress of its formative period."

There's clearly no question that the mineral wealth in northeastern Minnesota played an important and profitable role in the lives of many, many people. It's unfortunate more of them couldn't have been Minnesotans.

Chapter 7

In the few decades between 1858, when Minnesota became the nation's 32nd state, and the beginning of the Twentieth Century, the growth of business here was nothing short of phenomenal. The spurt was led, of course, by the timber industry, flour milling and activities on the Vermilion, Mesabi and Cuyuna iron ranges, all of which contributed to the furious pace of railroad construction. While these robust undertakings were being noticed around the country, there also was a silent upheaval going on in the Minnesota business community—a development which, in the aggregate, was bigger than any of the major industries.

Thousands of small businesses were started both to supply the needs of the growing flour mills, sawmills, iron mines and railroads, and to accommodate the mushrooming population in the new state. For present residents of Minnesota, who regard normal growth in this mature state as an increase of a few percentage points in a 10-year span, it's almost inconceivable to understand the excitement a century ago of a doubling in population in just a few years, and then doubling again. In the first federal census of 1860, the two-year-old state had 172,022 residents, most of them living around Minneapolis and St. Paul. By 1865, it was estimated that the state had grown to a population of about 258,000, and, by the next official census in 1870, there were 439,000 people living in Minnesota. The real growth, however, was to come in the next 20 years, as both new industry attracted workers and probably even more important some of the best farmland in the country became available. It sold for a couple of dollars an acre at the most, and some of it was free to homesteaders who "proved up" their claims to 160-acre parcels by living on them for five years.

By 1890, the population of Minnesota was 1,300,000, almost eight times the number just 30 years earlier. While the main population growth was in the rural areas, the major center of commerce remained the Twin Cities of Minneapolis and St. Paul. St. Paul, which had become the capital, was the larger of the two cities for several years, but, by 1890, Minneapolis, mostly because of its thriving flour industry, had outgrown its sister. The first census in 1860 showed St. Paul with 20,030 and Minneapolis with 13,066 residents. In 1890, Minneapolis had grown to 164,738, while St. Paul trailed at 133,156.

Servicing the needs and desires of this burgeoning population required all the ingenuity early entrepreneurs could muster, but it also presented ambitious businessmen with an opportunity that, unfortunately, has never been available since. Anyone with a few dollars of capital, an idea, and a desire to enter a business could set up shop within a day or two. Some of them didn't succeed, for the same reasons present businesses fail, but today's mortality of eight of every 10 companies within the first five years was a tragic fate still far off in the future.

To fully understand the relative ease of establishing a business in Minnesota in those early days, one must realize that practically everything was stacked in the entreprenuer's favor. There was such a demand for goods and services and so few people around with any business experience, that moving here from the East was a great temptation for hordes of entrepreneurs. Land was cheap; labor costs were ridiculously low; building supplies were abundant, and the term "government interference" had yet to be invented.

Because of its natural waterways and, later, the railroads, the Twin Cities area was especially attractive to early settlers. Ever since 1805, when a young army lieutenant, Zebulon Pike, bought the nine square miles of land that constitutes most of the present Minneapolis and St. Paul from the Sioux Indians for $200 and 60 gallons of whisky, the area at the junction of two important rivers had been a magnet for early settlers. With Fort Snelling providing protection, settlers could feel comfortable in building homes nearby. Growth was slow at first, but by 1840 St. Paul had been settled and, in 1850, took on the name it has today. St. Anthony became a community in 1855, and 10 years later Minneapolis was granted a charter as a city. St. Anthony became part of Minneapolis in 1872. Because most stores and other businesses prior to statehood in 1858 were small, little has been recorded about their ownership or activities. As the state began to mushroom in population, however, bigger businesses were started, and they spawned whole new industries in addition to the ones discussed in earlier chapters.

Before the railroads turned Minnesota into a year-around center of commerce, business followed an annual cycle, based primarily on river conditions. An editorial in the *Chronicle and Register,* a St. Paul newspaper, on March 30, 1850, clearly summed up the situation during the Spring doldrums: "But business is wretchedly dull in all our towns. The populace appears to be partaking of the quietude and calmness of the weather. They stand about the streets in isolated groups, practicing the pastime of the universal Yankee nation—whittling, and occasionally casting an anxious eye upon the surface of the river, as though they expected to see the ice smash to pieces, or the mail wending its way upward. The goods are all sold, the teams have finished their hauling to the North, the sleighing is over, the building season cannot actively commence as yet; and we are all waiting for something that is *going to happen.* We hope before many days, viz.: the opening of navigation. Save the eternal clatter of the millsaws at St. Anthony and along the St. Croix, the Territory is asleep.''

Once the rivers were free of ice and steamboats could travel again, the whittling stopped and commerce began. Business boomed until cold weather stopped the boats, and for several weeks until the ice on the rivers was thick enough to support the sleighs, Minnesotans went back to their whittling. River traffic actually began when the fur traders carried goods back and forth in their canoes, but it wasn't until 1823 that the first steamboat, the Virginia, reached Fort Snelling on May 10 after a 20-day journey from St. Louis, 730 miles to the south. The 118-foot sternwheeler demonstrated that it was practical to navigate the upper Mississippi River with big steamboats. The boats had to make several unscheduled stops en route, not only to get off the numerous sandbars they would invariably run on to, but also to replenish the supply of firewood needed to keep the boilers hot. The number of boats coming into the Twin Cities area increased every year after the Virginia opened the traffic until the peak was reached in about 1858 when more than a thousand boats were counted during the summer at the St. Paul levee. As railroads and wagon trails were established, the importance of river traffic diminished, but business, relieved of the ice-imposed annual slow-down, could flourish in pace with the soaring population.

Retail stores, supplying the variety of needs of the early settlers, were among the first businesses to open. Lumber sales to build the homes and businesses of the new communities were especially brisk. Banks and insurance companies opened; warehouses were needed; slaughter houses and meat markets sprang up, and food stores that bought directly from the farmers supplied the groceries for residents. Newspapers were also among the very first businesses to be established.

Besides helping to create an early sense of community, pioneer newspapers also became an important means of spreading the facts—and promises—about Minnesota to restless persons out East. James M. Goodhue, who arrived in St. Paul in April 1849 from Wisconsin, carried with him his own printing press, which he assembled almost immediately and started to produce a newspaper, the *Minnesota Pioneer*. Originally from New Hampshire, Goodhue devoted much of his newspaper to promoting Minnesota to a wide readership outside the territory. He was singularly responsible for attracting thousands of new residents. A vigorous, outspoken journalist, Goodhue established a fearsome reputation in the few short years he printed the *Pioneer*. He died in 1852, only five years after founding the newspaper, but, in that short time, he had become a powerful influence in the area.

Newspapers in those days were vastly different from today's rather timid chronicles, and editors needed to be strong fighters as well as good writers. An example of the type of writing dished out to early settlers can be found in an editorial by Goodhue about David Cooper, a territorial judge, who for some reason was disliked intensely by the editor. Part of Goodhue's scathing attack on Judge Cooper, printed in January 1851 in the *Pioneer,* reads: "He is not only a miserable drunkard, who habitually gets so drunk as to feel upward for the ground, but he also spends days and nights and Sundays playing cards in groceries. He is lost to all sense of decency and self respect. Off the bench, he is a beast, and on the bench, he is an ass, stuffed with arrogance, self conceit, and a ridiculous affectation of dignity."

The day after the offending editorial was printed, Joseph Cooper, brother of the judge, demanded a duel with Goodhue and the two men, armed with knives and guns, had an encounter on a St. Paul street. They survived the duel, but Goodhue was stabbed, Cooper was shot, and both required medical attention.

In the days before radio or television, with few books or magazines available, it was the newspaper that provided settlers with their only news of the outside world, and it was the newspaper that told the outside world about the glories of the Minnesota Territory. Goodhue was not above exaggeration when it came to descriptions of the territory he had come to love. He minimized the problems of Minnesota's weather by calling it a "fresh and bracing climate." He lured farmers here with the promise of "lands as fertile as the banks of the Nile," and he eliminated their fears of Indian attack by saying the Indians were "fading, vanishing, dissolving away." A graduate of Amherst College in the East, Goodhue was an educated writer with a clever knack for arranging a sentence to accomplish just about any purpose he had in mind. He painted a glowing picture of Minnesota because he, himself, was an optimist and he wanted others to enjoy the territory as he was. Goodhue was harsh on those he disagreed with, and that included large numbers of people, especially politicians. He hated dull speeches and described them being "as long as the ears of the human donkeys that get up and bray them."

Goodhue's *Pioneer* was the first newspaper to circulate in Minnesota, but, unlike some other industries, pioneer journalism was seldom a monopoly. Within 10 years from the time Goodhue started his publication, there were 89 newspapers in the territory, and the number continued to grow throughout the rest of the century, peaking at more than 700 by the early 1900s. Most of them, of course, local weeklies. In the early years of publishing, the production of a newspaper was only a part of the business, and commercial printing often produced more revenue for the editor than did the newspaper. The state's oldest printing concern is an offshoot of Goodhue's *Pioneer* and is still doing business today under the name of McGill/Jensen, Inc., in the Midway area of St. Paul. Charles H. McGill and his partner, Eli S. Warner, bought into the ownership of the *Pioneer*'s printing business and, by 1909, owned that phase of the operation completely, while the newspaper went on to become today's *St. Paul Pioneer Press* and *Dispatch.* McGill, the son of Andrew R. McGill, governor of Minnesota from 1887 to 1889, was one of the state's printing industry leaders. He introduced several innovations, including the first Monotype machine, which replaced tedious hand typesetting, and the first lithograph press. Today, organizational descendent of his commercial printing firm represents the merger of several companies, including Jensen Printing, Holden Printing, True-Color, and Printing, Inc.

The H.M. Smyth Printing Co., also still operating today, was founded in St. Paul in 1877 as a firm specializing in commerical printing without the benefit of a newspaper. H.M. Smyth, the founder, catered to the needs of other businesses in the Twin Cities, producing folders, invoices, calling cards and letterheads. As many new businesses became established in St. Paul and Minneapolis, there was an increasing need for printed materials, keeping Smyth's presses humming. The company outgrew its first two plants in less than 14 years and eventually moved into a new building of its own at Ninth and Temperance streets in St. Paul. G.G. McGuiggan, who started as a printer with the Smyth firm, became president and general manager in the early 1900s. He was succeeded by his son-in-law, William J. Hickey Sr., and Hickey's son, William J. Hickey Jr., is currently president, keeping control of the company in the same family for nearly 80 years.

Besides McGill and Smyth, dozens of other printers began operations in Minnesota during the last 25 years of the Nineteenth Century. Many of their firms still survive, and today the Twin Cities area is regarded as one of the top graphic arts centers of the entire nation. Much of the credit for this goes to the success of those pioneer printers, who saw the opportunity of growth during the bustling years of the late 1800s. Three early leaders in this field, the Webb Co., West Publishing Co., and Brown & Bigelow, are today giants in the industry, and although they all diversified as they grew, each started as a small printing or publishing concern in St. Paul between 1876 and 1896.

West, the oldest of the three, was founded by 24-year-old John B. West and his brother, Horatio, on Oct. 21, 1876. John West, an operator of a St. Paul book store specializing in law books and legal forms, saw a need for a system from which lawyers could get, quickly and accurately, a written account of decisions handed down by Minnesota judges. The method then being used was to wait until the busy judges could write each decision and get them printed and ultimately distributed to the attorneys. The West brothers began to publish a weekly report, called *The Syllabi,* with excerpts of all court decisions in the state. It cost attorneys only $3 annually to receive the eight-page pamphlet every week, and the response was so encouraging, the West brothers expanded into other states with the service.

Today, West Publishing Co., headquartered in a 10-story building on the banks of the Mississippi River in downtown St. Paul, reports on the more than 40,000 decisions handed down annually by the nation's federal courts and state appellate courts. Although neither of the West brothers was an attorney, many of the company's present 2,000 workers are lawyers, and the business has expanded into a variety of different publishing services for the nation's legal system. West, a privately owned company since its founding, has a virtual monopoly today in reporting and indexing court decisions for lawyers. Such dominance clearly indicates the satisfaction its customers have had with the service for more than a century. When the West brothers began operations, John was the salesman, selling subscriptions to attorneys and getting judges to send their decisions to him as quickly as possible, while Horatio, who was an accountant, handled the company's financial affairs. Their success owed much to their unique Key Number System, a method of indexing each case, which made looking up past decisions a much simpler process for lawyers. Today, attorneys throughout the country depend on West Publishing more than any other company for law books and legal reporting.

A more conventional printer and publisher, the Webb Co., founded in 1882, is now the largest printing concern between Chicago and the West Coast, and is one of the few in the country big enough to print the millions of income tax returns required each year by the federal government. It also prints the telephone directories for Northwestern Bell, in addition to dozens of four-color publications. When Edward A. Webb started the company, however, its only product was a publication for farmers in Minnesota, North and South Dakota. Called *The Farmer*, the biweekly periodical is still the company's flagship publication with circulation of nearly 190,000.

When 30-year-old Edward Webb started *The Farmer*, it was strictly a one-man operation, and although he was by training a journalist, the new business venture required that he also set type, run the press, sell advertising and distribute the publication. He was living in Fargo, N.D., when he got the idea for the magazine, but he soon moved to St. Paul to be closer to news sources at the University of Minnesota School of Agriculture. The company he began now has more than 1,000 employees with annual sales of about $80 million. Reuel Harmon, whose father was one of Edward Webb's early associates, is currently chairman of the board, while Robert Haugan is president and chief executive officer.

Another one-man printing operation that grew into a multi-million dollar corporation in St. Paul is Brown & Bigelow, now a diversified advertising specialty firm. Herbert H. Bigelow founded the company on Feb. 7, 1896, with the financial help of Hiram Brown. Each partner put up $2,000. Although Brown had no intention of becoming active in the company and soon withdrew, his name was never removed. Bigelow, who was 25 when he began the business, specialized in printing calendars for businesses, and that's still an important part of today's volume of nearly $70 million in annual sales. In his first year, however, Bigelow was able to generate only $13,000 in sales, hardly enough to meet his expenses and a small salary. Nevertheless, expansion came quickly for the industrious Bigelow, and he outgrew three locations in the first decade. By 1906, he bought the former Lexington race-track site, 17 acres in the Midway area of St. Paul. The location still served as the company's headquarters, though a move to new facilities is planned. Brown & Bigelow has enlarged its services from printing calendars into the manufacture of various types of advertising specialties, including desk and household accessories, playing cards, greeting cards, personal items, leather-bound books and novelties.

Herbert Bigelow's career, as successful as it was, was marred by misfortune and, finally, an untimely, mysterious death. A decade after Bigelow had turned the business from a one-man shop into a thriving operation, he was convicted of income tax evasion. While in Leavenworth federal prison, Bigelow met and became friendly with Charles A. Ward, who was serving time on a narcotics charge. Bigelow returned to manage his company after his release, and in 1925, when Ward was freed, Bigelow hired him as a factory apprentice at $25 a week. Ward rapidly progressed to the management level, and when Bigelow mysteriously drowned in Basswood Lake on the Minnesota-Canadian border during a fishing trip, Ward succeeded him as president.

Ward instituted a policy of hiring ex-convicts whenever possible, and the company earned a nationwide reputation as a rehabilitation center for former prisoners. Under Ward's imaginative guidance, the firm became a country's largest calendar manufacturer. The company even secured exclusive rights to photographs of the Dionne quintuplets during the peak of their popularity in the 1930s. His success at Brown & Bigelow and his program to help rehabilitate prisoners, earned Charles Ward a presidential pardon before his death. In 1970, the company was purchased by Saxon Industries, a New York-based conglomerate, and today operates as a successful division of its parent firm, accounting for about 10 percent of its overall business. (Brown & Bigelow is only one of dozens of Minnesota businesses, which over the years have found it advantageous to lose their independence to become part of a bigger, out-of-state company. But more about that later.)

The plethora of thriving printing firms that popped up in Minnesota during the late 1800s naturally led to the establishment of other graphic-arts companies needed to supply the various needs of the printers. Among them was the Buckbee Mears Co., still operating as a multi-million-dollar diversified manufacturer with worldwide sales. When it was founded by Charles E. Buckbee and Norman T. Mears, however, its only interest was in producing high quality photo-engravings for the printing trade. The two cousins, both in their late 20s, bought the St. Paul office of a Minneapolis printing and engraving firm, the Bureau of Engraving, Co., changed the name to Buckbee Mears Co. and began to build up a business of their own. The Bureau of Engraving, which had been started in Minneapolis in the late 1800s by Charles E. Buckbee's father, John Colgate Buckbee, was involved in photoengraving and general printing and even operated a correspondence school to train commercial artists and illustrators. The Bureau of Engraving is still operating in Minneapolis, and three generations of Buckbees have been involved in managing the successful firm. But back in 1907, the Bureau of Engraving, like many Minnesota companies, was suffering from a lack of operating capital because of the Panic of 1906. Charles Buckbee was already active in the company's St. Paul office, and he saw an opportunity to cut his ties with his father. He could set up shop for himself, if only he had the cash to buy part of the business. He approached his cousin, Norman T. Mears, and talked him into financing the purchase. On Aug. 16, 1907, the St. Paul branch of the Bureau of Engraving became the Buckbee-Mears Co., with Buckbee, who had the idea, assuming the presidency, and Mears, who put up the $3,200, which he borrowed from his father-in-law, becoming the new firm's secretary and treasurer. With five other workers, they started making metal engravings for printers, mostly on the St. Paul side of the river. They worked out of 1,500 square feet of space they rented in the Globe Building, a nine-story structure at Fourth and Cedar streets, a handy downtown location.

There was a strong demand from country weeklies throughout Minnesota for the zinc engravings used in those days to reproduce photographs, and Buckbee Mears soon became the prestige engraver for the region, doing a considerable amount of business for weekly newspapers not only in the state, but in Wisconsin, Iowa, North and South Dakota and even as far away as Montana. Always looking for ways to expand their business, the cousins capitalized on the proud feelings families had of their sons who fought in World War I and started what they called *County Books*. These publications contained a photo of and a paragraph about every young man who served in the military during the war. It was a profitable supplement to their engraving business. The company also got into the school annual field, and that remained an important operation until it was dropped in the 1930s. The imaginative company was the first in the entire Midwest to produce engravings for four-color printing and was one of the leaders in making photo-offset plates when they started to replace the more conventional printing methods.

The move out of the graphic arts into other fields came after Norman T. Mears' son, Norman Beebe Mears, joined the company in 1928. The son had originally decided to go into farming and had majored in animal husbandry at the University of Minnesota. After several years operating his own farm, he decided his father's photo-engraving business offered better opportunities, and with an investment of $7,000 saved during his farming career, Norman B. Mears bought into the family firm. Much of the diversification which came later was due to the son's ambitious planning and implementation. Using the same technological principles involved in engraving metal, N.B. Mears began producing components for optical devices. Today, Buckbee Mears, with third-generation members of the Mears family still active, is manufacturing precision etched and electro-formed products such as aperature masks for colored television sets, mesh for electron tubes, flexible circuitry for computer memory systems and multifocal ophthalmic lens blanks. With about 1,500 employees in plants in this country and in West German, Buckbee Mears sometime in the 1980s, will most likely exceed $100 million in sales, a far cry from the volume produced in the small engraving plant in downtown St. Paul at the beginning of this century.

Although records to substantiate it are lacking, it appears that the dozen years between 1880 and 1892 were perhaps more vibrant for Minnesota businesses than any other period in the state's history, with the possible exception of the boom years between the mid 1950s and 1969. Opportunities for entrepreneurs in the late 1800s were such that only the very weakest were threatened with failure. Thousands of businesses were started during those roaring years, and many of them are still existing. Capital was abundant and interest rates were low. The work force in Minnesota was plentiful, of extremely good quality and inexpensive. Demand for goods and services was high.

As usual, however, the exuberance of businessmen in Minnesota, and throughout the nation, led to excesses, and by early 1893, all the classic features of economic over-expansion were present. The time was ripe for a crash of some type, and the only thing lacking was an incident to trigger it. That came in May 1893, when a sudden withdrawal of U.S. gold by foreign investors precipitated a monetary crisis that led to one of the severest panics in the country's history. The whole nation suffered, and the bustling Minnesota business community was no exception. The infamous Panic of 1893 lasted throughout the year, and after-effects were felt for the remainder of the century. There were 642 bank failures in the United States that year, including dozens in Minnesota, and more than 15,000 businesses of all types went bankrupt. The panic was exceptionally severe for the highly leveraged railroad industry, and companies controlling more than one-third of all rail trackage in the country failed during the depression which followed the panic. The St. Paul-based Northern Pacific was among the 156 railroads which went into receivership. Of the several hundred small meat-packing firms which had started in Minnesota and other states west of the Mississippi River during the preceding 20 years, only four, including the Geo. A. Hormel Co. at Austin, Minn., survived the crash.

A dozen relatively large banks in the Twin Cities were forced to close, and countless smaller country banks could not endure the frantic runs on them by worried savers. Among the Twin Cities banks that failed were the National German American Bank, the Ramsey County Savings Bank, the Bank of Minnesota, the Germania Bank and the State Savings Bank of St. Paul. One of the few to weather the crisis was the Bank of Worthington, capably run by George Draper Dayton, who a few years later would move to Minneapolis to start the department store chain which today, as the Dayton Hudson Co., is one of the country's largest retailers. The Panic of 1893 was also cruel to real estate investors, farmers and those trading with the farmers. Every large farm mortgage company in Minnesota went out of business. Farm commodities suffered severely with the price of wheat plunging to 40 cents a bushel and oats dropping to 10 cents a bushel. Cows brought only $10 a head on the market, and sheep sold for as little as a dollar a head, less than the cost to transport them to market.

Businesses that survived the 1893 debacle demonstrated that they had the foundations established to withstand just about any adversity, and many of them are still doing business in Minnesota today. As one wag described the aftermath of the panic: "After a tornado has swept through an area, the trees which remain are regarded as first-class timber." Not only did the financial crisis weed out all but the strongest of businesses in Minnesota, it also provided the opportunity for others to begin. The most notable example of this was the establishment in 1894 of Investors Syndicate, known today as Investors Diversified Services, Inc., the largest financial institution of its type in the country. During the frantic days in 1893, a young Minnesota law student, John Tappan, realized there was a terrific opportunity for someone who could provide not only a safe haven for a person's hard-earned savings, but one which offered a better return and other advantages not available in the panic-shaken banking system. With total capital of only $2,500, Tappan started his new business on July 10, 1894, in a one-room office in the Lumber Exchange Building in downtown Minneapolis. His main asset was an idea that is still paying off nearly a century later. He had concluded, at the young age of 26, that individuals who had suffered the most during the recent economic crisis, and those who again would suffer in recessions yet to come, fell into one of two distinct categories: the thriftless, who spent as they went and put aside nothing for the future, and the thrifty who had saved something but lost their homes and savings during a depression.

Unusually astute for someone so young, Tappan's only work experience was a job collecting bad debts during the day while he studied law at night. He realized that the only way he could consistently collect long overdue debts was to help those who owed money set up a plan which included regular payments to eventually eliminate the obligation. Tappan figured if he could convice debtors of the necessity of organizing their financial matters, he should easily be able to show people not yet in trouble how to systematically save money to prevent future difficulties. The key to his plan was to penalize anyone who started a system and then, for any reason, didn't follow through. Banks and other savings institutions had no penalty for anyone wanting to withdraw money, and Tappan concluded this was not only a disservice to the saver, but also the main reasons so many banks had failed during the recent panic. If hysteric savers hadn't made runs on the banks to take out their money, most of the hundreds of banks which had to close the previous year would have been able to stay in business, Tappan correctly deduced.

After incorporating his Investors Syndicate, Tappan then wisely decided that he would have to go after the people to explain his plan; that no matter how badly people needed help with their financial planning, they would never come and ask for it. His next step was to find the best investment available in which he could put the money entrusted to him by his clients. By examining various investments by life insurance companies, banks and building and loan associations, Tappan learned that, during the past 50 years, the most secure and profitable venture was a first mortgage on a small home occupied by the owner and located in a major city. This had proved to be relatively safe, even during depressions. It was a well known fact that a wealthy investor with $5,000 or more could lend the money at a high rate of interest to someone who wanted to buy a home and get a good return at very little risk, because the entire property would revert to him in case of default. Tappan figured if he could get 1,000 people each to give him $5, he would have $5,000 with the same safety and yield the wealthy investor could get. Tappan set out selling investment certificates to individuals in the Twin Cities area. Certificate owners were required to make small, regular payments until the certificates matured in order to collect full interest premiums. The maturity time was usually 10 years. Within a year, Tappan had 150 contracts with individuals, and was slowly building his reserves. By the end of 20 years, his company had $88,000 in assets, and even though there had been two depressions during that time, every certificate had been paid promptly when due. The reputation of the firm as a safe and profitable depository for savings was being made throughout the area. By 1918, the company passed the $1 million mark in assets, and by 1925, when Tappan, then 57 years old, sold his interest in the company, Investors Syndicate had more than $12 million in assets.

John R. Ridgway purchased Tappan's company and he was joined in managing the company by E. M. Richardson and E.E. Crabb. The new owners continued Tappan's sound policies and expanded the company to all parts of the country with thousands of salesmen selling directly to individuals, mostly in small towns. The stability of Investors Syndicate was put to a test during the depression years of the 1930s, but while other financial institutions failed, it continued to grow. In 1929, Investors Syndicate had $29 million under management, and during the next 10 years paid out $101 million to certificate holders, always promptly and in full. By 1939, the company was managing $153 million.

Serious trouble, climaxed by charges of illegal practices by the federal Securities and Exchange Commission, beset the company during World War II. Operating under the stiff terms of a SEC consent decree, Investors Syndicate was wobbling and looking for new direction. However, Investors Syndicate found itself in this situation mainly as a result of actions taken by the U.S. government in its efforts to finance the war. Ceilings were put on most commercial interest rates that were lower than the interest rates that could be obtained on U.S. Savings Bonds. This was a strong encouragement to people to invest in Savings Bonds. However, because of the interest ceilings, Investors Syndicate could no longer obtain the interest rates on its investments that it had in the past, and which were necessary to cover Investors Syndicate's interest payments to its certificate holders, which were still at the old higher interest rates. Not surprisingly, this situation eventually depleted the Syndicate's reserves to the point where it operated for a time under a consent decree.

This situation constituted a ripe opportunity for another Minnesota entrepreneur, Bertin C. Gamble, founder of the profitable Gamble-Skogmo retailing empire. Gamble learned he could buy control of Investors Syndicate for only $650,000. He personally had $500,000 in cash, but needed another $150,000 to complete the deal.

Gamble, one of Minnesota's most colorful business figures who only recently stepped down as the operator of Gamble-Skogmo after more than a half century at the helm, tells how he quickly raised the money: "I had met Hal Roach Sr., the movie producer, on a New York trip and asked him if he had any money to gamble with. He said he had, so when this Investors Syndicate deal came up, I wired Roach in California and asked him for $150,000 without telling him what it was for. Within 30 minutes, I had a draft wired from the Culver City branch of the Bank of America from Roach. I then bought control of Investors Syndicate. A few days later, Hal Roach wrote me and said, 'Dear Bert, Isn't it about time you let me in on just a little bit of what's going on?' "

With the aggressive Gamble now operating the company, things began to improve although it should be pointed out that his timing was extreemely fortuitous. With World War II over, the interest rate ceilings were removed, and Investors Syndicate was able again to obtain the interest rates on its investments that enable it to make money, and to get out from under the consent decree. Gamble obtained the services of a top investment counselor, established a research department and expanded the investment policies by making direct industrial loans and construction loans. Gamble relates, "This put millions and millions of dollars into the company, and put it in the kind of reserve picture the SEC wanted. I did a lot of things to improve conditions at the company, but the folks at Gamble-Skogmo were beginning to complain I spent too much time at Investors Syndicate and not enough at Gamble-Skogmo, which wasn't doing too well at the time and Phil [Skogmo] was dying. I had to either sell one company or the other, so I tried to sell the Syndicate, but there wasn't one damn person in Minneapolis who would stick his neck out. I had to stay in and slug it out."

In 1949, Gamble found an interested buyer in Robert Young, who owned a New York company, the Alleghany Corp. Alleghany today is controlled by the Kirby family interests and the late Allan Kirby, who died in 1973, was a son of one of the five founders of the F.W. Woolworth Co. At the time Kirby was incapacitated by a stroke in 1967, he was the largest individual stockholder in F.W.

Woolworth. Negotiations were stalled for several months, however, because Gamble wouldn't say how much he wanted for Investors Syndicate, and Young wouldn't make an offer. Gamble remembers, "I'd left some financial statements with them and I wrote and asked for them back. They must have figured I was going to sell to someone else, because in eight days Young said he would buy my stock for $1,700,000. Within 30 days, the deal was made."

Gamble made a million dollars on the sale, a good return for a four-year old investment, but it was probably one of the worst decisions he has ever made. Had Gamble held control of the company, and had IDS shown the same growth it has registered under Alleghany ownership, Gamble's interest today would be worth several hundred million dollars. Alleghany, which built up its ownership in IDS by 1955 to 93.5 percent, nearly lost control of the firm in the early 1960s. Alleghany started to sell some of its holdings in IDS and the Murchison brothers in Texas became interested in taking control of the firm, losing to Alleghany only after a heated proxy battle. Gamble made a further effort to gain control of IDS by purchasing a large block of stock from the Murchisons in the early 1960s. He then approached Alleghany to see if they would be interested in the two of them acquiring complete control of IDS, but Alleghany was not interested. Gamble's IDS stock was eventually purchased from him by Alleghany. In 1979, Alleghany, which then owned 56 percent of the voting stock and 37 percent of the equity in IDS, decided it wanted all of the firm and planned to operate it as a wholly owned subsidiary. In May 1979, Alleghany completed the acquisition, paying about $198 million in cash and securities to buy what it didn't already own.

Gamble says about his 1949 decision, "Mrs. Gamble didn't want to sell, and she was right. But if you grieve over the past and worry about the future you're sure to go crazy."

Chapter 8

Bertin Gamble was fairly typical of the men who founded businesses in Minnesota during the late 1800s and the first part of the Twentieth Century—a period when survival in the corporate jungle was beginning to become tougher. The Panic of 1893 frightened many would-be entrepreneurs, and it prompted state and federal government officials to get more involved in the affairs of private enterprise. The laissez faire doctrine that had given free-wheeling businessmen a great amount of leeway was disappearing.

Gamble and his peers discovered that in addition to the aggressive traits earlier displayed by such Minnesota giants as J.J. Hill, John and Charles Pillsbury, Cadwallader Washburn and T.B. Walker, it was becoming necessary to be extremely imaginative and innovative to stay ahead of the competition. The state's abundant natural resources no longer were available for those who just had the pluck to go out and grab them. Cheap land was gone. Virgin timber stands were disappearing. The rich iron ore was firmly in the hands of the Eastern capitalists. As the new century began, Minnesota businessmen were learning that to succeed, one had to be more clever, shrewder and able to adapt to a new set of rules dictated by growing government concern that monopolies no longer should be encouraged.

So in building Gamble-Skogmo, with the help of Philip W. Skogmo, from its origins as an automobile dealership into the retailing and financial services giant it is today, Gamble had to deal with, and operate within the confines of, a whole set of governmental rules and regulations with which earlier entrepreneurs were unencumbered. In spite of these obstacles, when Bert Gamble, at age 79, reluctantly relinquished his iron-fisted control over the rambling company he had built on Sept. 20, 1977, Gamble-Skogmo had 3,144 outlets and sales of $1.6 billion.

Gamble was a restless individual, not satisfied unless dreaming up a new scheme or making a clever deal. Even as a youth in his hometown of Arthur, N.D., where his father was a banker, Gamble displayed signs of disquietude. When his father died in 1915, young Gamble, who was then 17, moved to Minneapolis with his mother and enrolled in a business college to learn typing and shorthand. He quit after three months and took a job as a bookkeeper and stenographer at the Dairy Supply Co. in Minneapolis, a position, incidentally, made available to him through a North Dakota schoolmate, Phil Skogmo, who was working as a salesman at the firm. Skogmo was later to become Gamble's partner, and the relationship lasted until Skogmo's death in 1949. Gamble stayed in this job for two years until he had saved enough money to buy a run-down farm near Beaulieu, for $2,700. At the age of 18, he was in business for himself. Recalling his farming experience, Gamble said, "The stock hadn't been taken care of; the cattle could hardly walk, and the pigs had rheumatism, but there was plenty of grain. Within a year, I fattened up the stock, painted the wagons and machinery red, oiled up the harnesses, doped up the horses and sold out at auction, netting a $1,600 profit."

With the profits from the farm, Gamble bought an ice cream parlor in Montevideo, the Palace of Sweets, and within five months sold it for a gain of $1,000. It was a tragic tornado at Fergus Falls, in the summer of 1919 that resulted in the Bertin Gamble-Phil Skogmo partnership. The twister killed 50 people at Fergus Falls, including the owner of the Hudson-Essex auto agency there. Months later, the dealership was still without an operator, so in March 1920, Gamble and Skogmo pooled their resources and, for an investment of $10,000, acquired the Hudson-Essex agency. During their first five years, the men sold the original agency, bought a larger garage and the Fergus Falls Dodge dealership, then the town's Ford agency and, by 1925, also owned auto agencies at Detroit Lakes and Montevideo, and Wahpeton, N.D.

Never content, Gamble was soon toying with the idea of getting out of auto sales and concentrating exclusively on auto parts, which proved to have higher profitability than the cars themselves. On March 11, 1925, the two men opened a retail automotive accessory store at St. Cloud, under the Gamble name. Within 10 weeks, they added similar stores at Fargo, N.D.; Grand Forks, N.D.; Aberdeen, S.D., and Sioux Falls, S.D. Their retailing empire was begun. So successful were the auto parts stores, the two men sold their car agencies, and by 1928, they had incorporated Gamble, Skogmo, moved their headquarters to Minneapolis and were operating 55 stores in five states.

Gamble's creative mind was always churning. In 1929 when he discovered that nearly half of the tires stocked in their various stores were odd-sized and slow movers, he had them all shipped to Minneapolis, where he rented a vacant building and advertised that Gambles was selling two tires for the price of one. This first two-for-one sale in the nation resulted in a complete sell-out in a single day. Clever promotions were constantly aborning in Gamble's fertile mind. He amazed his competition when he started buying radiator alcohol by the freight carload and selling a $1 size of antifreeze for only 44 cents. His stores sold five carloads in a single sale. Gamble demonstrated time and again the tremendous advantages large-scale buying had in the retail market.

His most successful promotion, which took place in 1959, involved negotiating with a freezer manufacturer to buy 100,000 of a single home freezer unit if the manufacturer would lower his price enough so that Gambles could sell them for $199 instead of the regular $300 price. To reduce costs, the freezers were shipped direct to key geographic distribution points and each retail store received one unit to display. In some instances customers went directly to the railroad yard and picked up their unit "in the crate" from the boxcar. "We sold 43,000 freezers in four months where we'd only sold 19,000 in the entire 12 months the year before," Gamble remembers. "It opened our eyes. It showed us we could move. We could do things BIG."

The freezer promotion also marked the company's first use of national advertising, with full-color ads appearing in Life, Look, The Saturday Evening Post and Successful Farming. Another feature of this sale was the company's offer to take in on trade any item of merchandise that was considered to be resaleable.

When the Great Depression startedbin 1929, and businesses of all types faltered, with many failing, Gambles continued merrily along expanding each year. The Gamble-Skogmo company opened more than 100 new company-owned stores between 1929 and 1933, increasing total sales from $5 million to $10 million. It was in 1933 that the company entered the franchise business, largely because of the many inquiries it received from individuals who wanted to sell Gambles merchandise in their own stores, and also because it meant that new stores could be opened at a faster rate. In response to this interest, the Gambles Authorized Dealer Plan was developed. Although the program offered few of its present advantages, 380 Dealer Stores were opened during 1933—a startling achievement for a year of overall depressed business activity.

Bert Gamble grew tired, though, of the slow process of opening new stores. His patience was wearing thin even though his switch to the franchise system in 1933, by which time Gambles was selling hardware items, paint and tools, as well as auto supplies, made it easier and faster to add outlets. His solution to expanding the number of Gamble-Skogmo outlets faster was to find other chains of similar stores and to buy the entire company.

Gamble's first target was the large Western Auto Supply network. There were two separate companies, one located in Los Angeles and another in Kansas City. In 1939, Gamble and Skogmo bought controlling interest in the Los Angeles operation for $2 million, adding another 300 stores to the Gamble chain. When they tried to acquire the larger Kansas City operation, however, the federal government stepped in and prevented the sale on the grounds it would lessen competition in the Midwest states where both Gambles and Western had stores. Never one to admit defeat, Gamble turned around and sold his Western Auto of Los Angeles to the Kansas City company for $10 million, giving him a profit of $8 million. Then he had a friend in Canada, Robert O. Denman, quietly buy control of the entire Western Auto operation in the open market. When that was accomplished, Gamble bought the Canadian's interest in Western Auto for $26 million and completed his dream of owning the firm.

The U.S. Justice Department wasn't fooled, however, and started action again against Gamble. It took two years, but Gamble was finally forced to divest his Western Auto control, which he did by selling his shares to Beneficial Finance Co. of Wilmington, Del., for an inflated price of $51 million, giving the shrewd Gamble a quick profit of $25 million.

In some of his later years, Gamble made as much profit buying and selling companies as he did operating his retail network. He had an uncanny eye for corporate bargains. He bought 40 percent interest in Investors Syndicate of Canada Ltd., for $8.8 million, only to see the stock double in value in just two years. Probably Gamble's biggest bargain was his purchase of the Red Owl Stores, headquartered in Hopkins. He bought 78 percent of the food company's common stock for $28.7 million, which was less than half the firm's book value. Today Red Owl is an important contributor to the Gamble-Skogmo financial statement.

Other acquisitions while Gamble was still in power included Aldens of Chicago, the country's fifth largest mail order merchandising catalog company; two Canadian department store chains, MacLeods of Winnipeg and Stedmans of Toronto; the Snyder Drug Store chain, based at Hopkins, Mode O'Day of Burbank, Calif.; J.M. McDonald's of Hastings, Neb.; Woman's World, LaMesa, Calif., and Rasco of Burbank, Calif. Gamble also directed the strategy which led the company into financial services.

Two more retail outlet acquisitions were made during 1978—Leath-Maxwell, home furnishing stores, Chicago, and Howard's Brand, discount stores, Monroe, La. All of the acquisitions of course are in addition to the approximately 1000 general merchandise stores in the Gamble stores division, of which over 900 are dealer-owned.

Gamble-Skogmo's stake in the financial services business continued to grow dramatically in 1978 with the merger of Aristar, Inc. Early in 1979, four of Gambles' financial services subsidiaries—Gamble Alden Life Insurance Co., Gamble Alden Agency, Gambles C & M Leasing Co., and Gambles International Leasing Corporation—were merged into Aristar which now serves as the corporate entity encompassing all financial services activities. Also included in Aristar is Blazer Financial Services division which operates consumer financial offices.

Bert Gamble, who was often called the Main Street Merchant, was one of the first to combine groceries, drugs and hardware into a one-stop shopping complex. He was also a financier and negotiator who completed many complex acquisitions in both the retail and financial service areas.

Critics of Gamble have called him dictatorial, egocentric and manipulative, but the traits a man must have to take a company from scratch to nearly $2 billion in sales in a half century must also certainly include his stark determination, his cunning ability to promote and his shrewd business sense.

Although unfettered free enterprise was a thing of the past as Minnesota businessmen were saying goodby to the 19th Century, there still remained exceptional opportunity for those with a new product or a new service that filled a need. William R. Sweatt, who was making a comfortable living building wooden wheelbarrows in Minneapolis, found himself with a new product so revolutionary, no one wanted to buy it. The story of Sweatt and his thermostat, a device to control indoor temperatures, is the story of how one of the state's major corporations, Honeywell, Inc., got started.

Sweatt didn't design the thermostat, but he was the one person who had the determination—and the capital—to see that this new product would find acceptance. The automatic thermostat, which today is found in every home and business in the modern world, was invented by a Minneapolis man, A.M. Butz, in 1885, but the company organized to sell the instrument, the Consolidated Temperature Controlling Co., failed. It was reorganized in 1889 and renamed the Electric Thermostat Co. It was that firm which approached Sweatt, asking him for desperately needed financing. The device was a hand-wound, spring-powered motor that controlled indoor temperatures by opening and closing a flapper draft on a coal-fired furnace or boiler. Sweatt immediately saw possibilities in this new device, which was a bit surprising for a manufacturer of wheelbarrows, a product that had enjoyed wide acceptance for hundreds of years.

Sweatt agreed to invest $1,500 in the company, but wanted no part in managing the firm, other than serving on the board of directors. The fledgling company, unable to convince homeowners the "new contraption" would make their lives any easier, went from one financial crisis to another with Sweatt bailing it out each time with new capital. The Panic of 1893 proved too heavy a burden for the Electric Thermostat Co., and the operators were ready to call it quits, unless, of course, Sweatt would agree to a reorganization which not only called for additional financing from him, but a commitment that he would get personally involved in running the firm. Already more heavily involved financially than he had ever planned to be, Sweatt agreed to become secretary-treasurer of a new company, the Electric Heat Regulator Co., and to take an active part in management without pay. He closed the company's office in the Temple Court Building in downtown Minneapolis, and moved the operations into his wheelbarrow plant at 32nd Avenue South and East 26th Street. Sweatt's efforts in the next few years kept the new company from losing money, and he even agreed to take a small salary in 1896, but there was little progress in gaining widespread acceptance for the thermostats. Keeping his wheelbarrow plant profitable demanded much of Sweatt's time, and, by 1898, another financial crisis confrontedbthe Electric Heat Regulator Co.

Sweatt had had it. He told the firm's directors he had writer's cramps from signing bank notes and his vest buttons were "worn smooth from rubbing against bank counters." In despair, the other stockholders told Sweatt he could have 100-percent ownership of the firm for $5,000, the amount the company's physical assets were worth. The money could be paid out of profits in excess of $25 a month, if there were any profits. Reluctantly, Sweatt agreed, but he apparently wasn't overly optimistic, because he retained his steady wheelbarrow business, too. However, he was spending most of his time with the thermostat, personally tramping the streets, selling the damper regulators to anyone with the slightest interest. He was able to show a small profit and slowly paid off the $5,000, gaining full ownership by retiring the debt in 1902. At that time he disposed of his wheelbarrow business and began devoting all his time and energy to making the regulator company succeed.

Sales growth was exceedingly slow, but they began to pick up in 1905 when Sweatt designed a timeclock for the thermostat, allowing a homeowner to turn down the heat at night and have it automatically go up an hour or so before he got out of bed. Homeowners were finally beginning to see the advantages of installing thermostats. The company expanded into a larger factory building at the corner of Lake Street and Portland Avenue in 1906; additional machinery was installed, and, before long, there were 12 full-time employees making damper motors from scratch and assembling thermostats from parts bought in the East. Sweatt's aggressive advertising and merchandising policies were beginning to bear fruit. In 1912, a new factory was built at Fourth Avenue and 28th Street, the first unit of a complex that ultimately was to cover the entire block. That same year, the capital stock of the company was increased to $200,000, and the name changed to the Minneapolis Heat Regulator Co.

A capable, hard-working crew contributed greatly to the company's progress. Starting pay for Sweatt's workers was 16½ cents an hour, with the average only 22 cents, and top pay—for a skilled tool maker—was 45 cents. The shop worked from 7 a.m. to 6 p.m., with 30 minutes for lunch, no coffee breaks, from Monday through Friday, and from 7 a.m. to 1 p.m. on Saturday for a total work week of 58½ hours. Sales by 1916 were $300,000 a year, and offices were opened in Boston, Chicago, Cleveland, Detroit, St. Louis, St. Paul, Springfield, Mass., and Syracuse, N.Y. There was even a Canadian sales office in Toronto. The Minneapolis Heat Regulator Co. was finally on its way.

William Sweatt's two sons, Harold Wilson Sweatt and Charles Baxter Sweatt, both joined the company following their schooling, Harold in 1913 and Charles in 1916. Harold Sweatt played a key role in one of the company's most important decisions in its early years. The firm's top competitor was the Honeywell Heating Specialties Co., located at Wabash, Ind. Since its founding in 1906, Honeywell had been taking a large share of the market away from the Sweatt operations. So fierce was the competition that William Sweatt would not speak to Mark Honeywell, the Indiana company's owner. It appeared that a merger of the firms would be of mutual advantage, but the owners so heartily disliked each other, negotiations were out of the question. Clever maneuvering by Harold Sweatt, however, broke the barrier, and, in 1927, the two companies joined forces, changing the name to the Minneapolis-Honeywell Regulator Co., keeping the headquarters in Minneapolis. It was not only the most significant development up to that time for both firms, but it also helped the merged company survive the coming depression.

Sales in 1928 for Minneapolis-Honeywell were $5.2 million, and despite the ravages of the Great Depression, the firm continued to grow. With the help of four other acquisitions, sales climbed to $19 million by 1940. The company had manufacturing plants in Minneapolis, Wabash, Ind., Philadelphia, Chicago and Elkhart, Ind. The Minneapolis plant had been enlarged four times by 1942. Harold Sweatt and Mark Honeywell took charge of the company after William Sweatt's death in 1937, and diversification into several other fields came swiftly. By 1950, sales exceeded the $100-million mark for the first time, and, 17 years later, they passed the $1 billion figure. Today, Honeywell has annual revenues of more than $3 billion and a total workforce exceeding 80,000 people with facilities throughout the world. In addition to its automatic-controls business, which now includes not only thermostats but controls of all types, the company is one of the largest computer manufacturers in the country. The gargantuan size of Honeywell, Inc., today was an unthinkable possibility to William Sweatt back in the days he was going door to door trying to peddle a new "contraption" to control indoor temperatures, but it certainly was his determination in those early years that made today's giant corporation possible.

There was plenty of opportunity in the Minnesota business community around the turn of the century, even for those companies without a new product or service, provided they could come up with an idea to fill a need. Bert Gamble had proved that retail chains were here to stay, and the tremendous advantages of large-scale buying threatened the small, independent store operator— regardless of the types of goods involved. If Gamble's chain of hardware stores worked, the chain principle would likewise work for food stores, as the development of huge supermarket networks later proved.

Independent retail grocers were predominant as the 20th Century began, but their days were numbered, because food buying for most consumers was strictly a matter of price. The store that could offer standard quality at a lower price won the customers. Food chains, which could buy in quantity and therefore obtain a lower price, could sell for less and still make a good profit. In addition, they could advertqse through the mass media to large numbers of potential customers, spreading the cost among many stores. These two considerable advantages would have meant certain doom for most independent operators if shrewd wholesale grocers hadn't come up with an idea to beat the chains at their own game.

Twin Cities-based Super Valu Stores, Inc., which is now the country's largest wholesale food operation, was one of the earliest to recognize the threat of retail chains, and among the first to develop strategy to combat the growing competition. Today, Super Valu sells food and non-food items to more than 2,000 independent grocers in two dozen states at prices that are competitive with those available to even the largest supermarket chains. In 1979, Super Valu, which now sells clothing and general merchandise as well as groceries, had annual sales exceeding $3 billion, making it one of Minnesota's largest businesses.

Super Valu traces its beginnings to the pioneer Minneapolis wholesale grocery firms of B.S. Bull and Co. and Newell and Harrison Co., both of which started back in the 1870s. Super Valu's direct predecessor was Winston and Newell Co., formed in 1926 as the result of a series of smaller mergers. It was founded primarily to improve service to struggling independent retailers who were about to give up the losing battle against the surge of chain store retailers in the 1920s. Winston and Newell added considerable strength to its campaign in 1928 when it affiliated with the Independent Grocers Alliance (IGA). Independent grocers were now able to compete effectively with the chains by grouping together, not only to buy most of their goods but also to achieve a unified identity that gave them cooperative promotional and advertising advantages.

The corporate name was changed to Super Valu in 1954, and the acquisition of several more regional wholesale distributors during the next dozen years greatly expanded the operations. New additions to the Super Valu family during that period included J.M. Jones Co., Champaign, Ill.; Food Marketing Corp., Ft. Wayne, Ind.; Chastain-Roberts Co., Anniston, Ala., and Lewis Grocer Co., Indianola, Miss. The company entered the food-processing industry in 1938, and, in 1960, it began distributing its products under the Super Valu label. The purchase of Institutional

Wholesaler Grocers, Inc., Des Moines, Iowa, in 1965 and the Minneapolis Restaurant Supply Co., in 1968 took the company into the institutional field. Super Valu broadened its scope to non-food merchandising in 1971 with the acquisition of Shop-Ko Stores, Inc., Green Bay, Wis., a self-service discount department store. In 1973, a casual-apparel division was started with the opening of five County Seat Stores. The company now has more than 200 of these ready-to-wear outlets in 33 states. The success of Super Valu is a textbook example of how Minnesota businessmen used clever ideas to cope with the changing times.

The concept of small businesses banding together to fight competition as a strong, effective group instead of struggling as disorganized individuals was by no means limited to the experiences of Super Valu. The entire farm cooperative movement was nothing more than another application of group power. Minnesota was the leader in the nation in establishing the success of farm co-ops, and Land O'Lakes, the Minneapolis-based giant with $2 billion in annual sales today, was the organization that started it all. The idea which gave Land O'Lakes its start in Minnesota goes back to 1891 when Professor Theophilus Levi Haecker, an outspoken teacher at the University of Minnesota farm school, traveled throughout the rural areas of the state, telling farmers they would never successfully market their butter if they didn't band together as a group. Haecker, who was to become known as the "father of cooperative creameries," dedicated his life to the idea.

The basic philosophical and organizational principles were already established, and a few cooperatives existed in Minnesota and other rural states, but the idea did not really catch on until Haecker started his one-man campaign. By the time Haecker retired in 1918, the Minnesota cooperative had made great progress, and co-ops had been formed throughout the state. Unfortunately, destructive competition and jealousy developed among many of them, and caused as many problems as the movement had been intended to solve. The first significant change came with the formation of the Meeker County Creamery Association in 1920, with a young Litchfield farmer, John Brandt, elected as president. This group decided cooperation with other cooperative organizations was absolutely necessary if the system was to work. A year later, the Meeker County group changed its name to Minnesota Cooperative Creameries Association, Unit No. 1, and invited other co-ops to join together in a statewide creamery federation.

This was the group that eventually became Land O'Lakes, an organization that proved to farmers they could do with dairy products what they had failed to do with wheat, that is, keep a good share of the profit with the producers instead of seeing most of it go to middlemen. The first 11 farmer-owned creameries to join Unit No. 1 of the association were located at Litchfield, Lake Stella, Dassel, Darwin, Kingston, Forest City, Grove City, Crow River, Danielson, Cosmo and Star Lake. Over the years, the organization has grown so that now Land O'Lakes has nearly 900 local cooperatives, representing more than 150,000 farmers under its umbrella.

In the beginning, the idea was to get a fair price for the farmers at the local creameries, but this soon spread to the necessity of better marketing of their products, originally limited to butter. Minnesota farmers were aware that their butter had won more first prizes in national buttermakers' contests than butter from all other states combined. Yet, in the marketplace, Minnesota butter was selling no better than inferior products. On April 23, 1921, a meeting was held in St. Paul of creamery representatives, and President John Brand of the Meeker County organization summed up the group's challenge: "We have in the past as cooperative creameries been centering our efforts in production lines. We have put forth our best efforts to produce the product and completely forgotten the marketing end of the game. I think the time is fast approaching when it is going to be necessary to organize a statewide association to market our products whether we want it or not."

Brand organized a marketing effort under the aegis of the Minnesota Cooperative Creameries Association, and, by February 1922, 310 creameries had signed on as members. The concept of farmers selling their own butter was not greeted with enthusiasm by the companies that previously dominated the marketing field, and one Eastern firm, the Fox River Butter Co., even ran a series of advertisements that attacked the farmers' "new and absurd theories." The Blue Valley Creamery Co. of Chicago tried to prevent the cooperative marketing plan by trying to buy the Sauk Lake Cooperative Creamery at Sauk Centre, Minn., but the offer was quickly turned down. In defiance, the Blue Valley firm opened a competing creamery in Sauk Centre and announced it was only the first of a series it would build in the state to fight the co-op movement. Minnesota farmers, however, refused to abandon the cooperative idea, and the Blue Valley invasion failed.

Before the Minnesota Cooperative Creameries Association could effectively market butter, a name for the product was the top priority, and the imaginative farmers decided to solve this problem by conducting a statewide contest to select an appropriate brand name. Offering a prize of $500 in gold, the co-op ran full-page advertisements in newspapers around the state, and nominations poured in at the rate of 7,000 letters a day. The winner, of course, was "Land O'Lakes," and, surprisingly, two different persons had suggested the same name. They split the prize. In 1926, after the association had expanded into Wisconsin and North and South Dakota, the brand name was also adopted for the organization, which became Land O'Lakes Creameries, Inc. Later, when the organization began to market other farm products, the word "creameries" was dropped.

In its early years, Land O'Lakes had its warehouse and office in St. Paul, but, as its quarters became crowded, it was necessary to move, and a sharp group of Minneapolis businessmen, realizing the possibilities of having the co-op in their city, put together a $350,000 bond issue to finance a large, modern building near the northeast edge of the city. The two-story, 400-by-100-foot building was dedicated on March 10, 1926, as Land O'Lakes' new home. Minnesota Gov. Theodore Christianson, said at the ceremony: "Cooperative marketing has passed its infancy and is now in the stage of fighting maturity." The governor probably never dreamed that Land O'Lakes, within another half-century would become a multi-billion dollar organization. Reflective of its origins, Land O'Lakes is still marketing butter, of course, but is now processes raw agricultural materials into a wide range of food products, including not only butter, but ice cream, dry milk, cheese, turkeys and dozens of other items. It also furnishes farmer members with livestock feed, seed, fertilizer, chemicals, petroleum products and other merchandise. It processes and markets soybean oil and meal. In 1978, it entered the red meat industry by acquiring Spencer Foods, Inc., an Iowa meat packer.

The colorful histories of Gamble-Skogmo, Honeywell, Super Valu and Land O' Lakes are just a few of the interesting stories of Minneosta business during the productive years of the late 1800s and the early 1900s. To adequately cover all the corporations which started in that period would be an impossibility in a single book. Not only did thousands of businesses begin in the Twin Cities and throughout the state, but whole new industries got started.

The telephone and the electric light gave life to such giants today as Northwestern Bell Telephone Co., Northern States Power and many other successful utility companies in the state. The first automobile was sold in Minnesota in 1903, and within two decades, the Ford Motor Co. was assembling vehicles in a large plant in St. Paul. The brewing industry spawned several large beer producers in the Twin Cities and hundreds in smaller communities throughout the state. Financial institutions expanded, with two of the country's largest bank holding companies, the First Bank System and Northwest Bancorporation, establishing headquarters in Minneapolis. The savings and loan industry started, giving birth to Twin City Federal Savings and Loan and Midwest Federal Savings and Loan. The meat-packing industry became one of the state's most important assets, with the Geo. A. Hormel Co. starting in Austin and the Armour plant opening in South St. Paul, making the South St. Paul Livestock Market one of the nation's largest.

Manufacturing served notice it would soon replace agriculture as the state's major source of income. Companies such as 3M, American Hoist & Derrick, U.S. Bedding, Paper, Calmenson & Co., Northern Malleable Iron and hundreds of other smaller manufacturing firms opened for business. Retailers led by Dayton's, Donaldson's, Field-Schlick, Juster's and other home-grown merchandisers began to grow from one-man stores to large organizations. The trucking industry produced firms like Murphy Transfer & Storage.

Minnesota probably will never see another era as exciting and fruitful for business as it was around the turn of the century.

Chapter 9

Down through the years, Minnesota business leaders had learned to expect periodic financial disasters—crashes, panics, recessions and depressions—and like agile cats, the stronger companies always seemed to land on their feet, wiser and more cautious but ready for the next crisis. The panics of 1837, 1857, 1873, 1893, 1906, and 1920 had prepared Minnesota businessmen for the hard, cruel fact of life that every few years the bottom seemed to fall out of their corporate basket.

So, the crash which shook the country in October 1929 wasn't totally unexpected. Many people felt, however, that it was a panic which only affected the shaky stock market, and that business in general wouldn't suffer as it had in the past when most panics started with bank failures. A brazen editorial in the *Minneapolis Tribune* in late October 1929 summed up the feeling of many corporate leaders of those days: "Outstanding in connection with the spectacular downward trend of the stock market is the clearly established fact that the fundamental business situation is sound and in no jeopardy because of current developments in the stock market. Legitimate business is unaffected."

That view was typical of many optimistic businessmen at the beginning of every financial downturn, so, as the country entered the 1930s, there was still debate going on, in Minnesota and throughout the nation, over whether this latest crash would ever filter down to the ordinary businessman.

What no one could have even suspected during those dark days on Wall Street in the last few months of 1929 and the early months of 1930 was that not only was this going to be a full-blown business depression, but that it would be the longest and most severe in history. So much attention was being paid to the strange events occurring in the stock market, that few businessmen were taking the time to make plans for the 10 tough years to follow.

Of the millions of words which have been written about the Great Depression of the 1930s, nothing seems more aptly descriptive than a statement made by economist John Kenneth Galbraith in his book, *The Great Crash 1929:* "A common feature of all these earlier troubles [previous depressions] was that, having happened, they were over. The worst was reasonably recognizable as such. The singular feature of the great crash of 1929 was that the worst continued to worsen. What looked one day like the end proved on the next day to have been only the beginning. Nothing could have been more ingeniously designed to maximize the suffering, and also to insure that as few as possible escaped the common misfortune. The fortunate speculator who had funds to answer the first margin call presently got another and equally urgent one, and if he met that there would still be another. In the end all the money he had was extracted from him and lost. The man with the smart money, who was safely out of the market when the first crash came, naturally went back in to pick up bargains. The bargains then suffered a ruinous fall. Even the man who waited out all of October and all of November, who saw the volume of trading return to normal and saw Wall Street become as placid as a produce market, and who then bought common stocks would see their value drop to a third or a fourth of the purchase price in the next 24 months.''

Galbraith's observation clearly sizes up the strange situation. No one could even dream such bad times could even become worse, or that depressed conditions could last so long. It took a while for Minnesota businessmen to even acknowledge that this crash would affect them. Then, when they finally accepted the fact, they kept looking for the end when the real beginning was still ahead.

Oct. 24, 1929, was the first day of the infamous stock market crash, and to many Minnesotans, it was regarded as only a well deserved kick in the pants for the nations' super wealthy. In retrospect, however, it was the ordinary people who suffered the most. There were 25 million people—stockholders and their families—who were wiped out in the crash, and only a small percent were the really wealthy. Within weeks of the so-called Black Thursday there were hundreds of thousands of workers laid off, and during the next four years, an average of 100,000 people lost their jobs every week until the unemployment total reached 20 m i l l i o n .

The first frightening evidence in Minnesota that perhaps the stock market crash would indeed affect business conditions in the state came on Saturday, Nov. 2, 1929, with the news that Wilbur B. Foshay, a prominent Minneapolis businessman with vast holding in a dozen states, was bankrupt. Everyone in Minnesota knew Foshay, if for no other reason that because of the spanking new 32-story Foshay Tower, that rose majestically some 400 feet above Eighth Street and Marquette Avenue in downtown Minneapolis.

The tallest skyscraper in the state, the Foshay Tower had been dedicated in an elaborate three-day ceremony only two months earlier. Foshay had hired John Philip Sousa and his 75-member marching band for the dedication. Sousa, who was paid $20,000 for his appearance (a check in that amount was dropped from the top of the tower by Foshay to the musician below), wrote the "Foshay Tower March" for the occasion, and played it for the 20,000 spectators who attended the celebration. Foshay also gave gold watches to his special guests, including President Herbert Hoover's personal envoy, Secretary of War James W. Good, who hailed the unusual obelisk as the "Washington Monument of the Northwest." Minnesota Governor Theodore Christianson praised the rotund, dynamic Foshay as one of the state's most brilliant business leaders.

Foshay spared no expense in constructing the towering $3,750,000 building. He even patented the method of construction, fabricated steel hot-riveted to reinforced concrete. The design could withstand winds of more than 400 miles an hour. Sienna marble and African mahogany was used throughout the interior. High-speed elevators rose 750 feet a minute. It was a glorious climax to the business career of a man who had come to Minnesota only 14 years earlier as a penniless entrepreneur, possessing only a dream. Within a decade, Foshay had built a $20-million enterprise that included utility companies in 12 states, Canada, Mexico and Central America. He also owned an assortment of banks, hotels, flour mills and manufacturing and retail establishments in Minnesota and other states.

Foshay was highly leveraged and heavily involved in the stock market. When the market crashed, he was one of the first to be crushed, and before 1929 ended, he not only lost all his possessions but faced an additional $1.5 million in debt he couldn't cover. His survival had depended almost wholly on his amazing ability to sell public stock in his various enterprises at inflated prices. When stock prices collapsed and the market dried up, the major source of his earnings vanished almost overnight.

The Post Office became interested in just how Foshay had been able to sell so much stock to the public, and an investigation showed violations of postal laws. Foshay was indicted on charges of using the mails to defraud in connection with the sale of securities, and in 1932, he was sentenced to 15 years at Leavenworth Federal Prison. It was obvious that Foshay had been caught up in the speculative fever of the late 1920s and was more guilty of greed than fraud. A campaign by his friends to have him pardoned began shortly after his imprisonment, and by 1937, after Foshay had served five years, his sentence was commuted, and he was freed. President Harry Truman finally pardoned him in 1947. Foshay died in obscurity in Minneapolis on Sept. 4, 1957, of a stroke at the age of 76.

His 1929 bankruptcy had, however, served as a warning to optimistic Minnesotans that the effects of the stock market crash weren't confined to Wall Street and New York. One of the first groups to feel the crushing blows of the financial disaster was the farmer. Cash income of Minnesota farmers plunged by more than 75 percent from 1929 to 1932, and as they were forced to stop spending, the state's entire economy suffered. The cash price for wheat in Minnesota dropped sharply from $1.21 a bushel to 49 cents, while corn fell from 78 cents a bushel to 21 cents.

Unemployment hit Minnesota hard, especially outside the metropolitan area. By the fall of 1932, more than 70 percent of the Iron Range workers were jobless. Relief costs soared, going from a negligible amount in 1929 to more than $9 million in 1933, and then to $33 million the following year. Grasshopper plagues and a severe drought added to the woes of farmers in the state.

The unrest in Minnesota during the early 1930s was an ideal atmosphere for labor problems, even violence. Those without jobs were naturally bitter, while those with jobs were being asked repeatedly to take pay cuts as business conditions worsened. Successful strikes by a Twin Cities upholsterers' union and then by another for coal-yard employees set the stage for one of the most bitter labor confrontations the state had ever experienced. Teamsters Local No. 574, seeking union recognition for Minnesota truck drivers, struck in May 1934, halting most truck deliveries in the Twin Cities. A Citizen's Alliance was formed with 500 volunteers opposed to union recognition, and in the next few months, there were several outbreaks of violence involving the strikers, members of the alliance, the National Guard and police. Before the summer was over, Governor Floyd B. Olson declared martial law, the union headquarters was raided by the National Guard with several labor leaders arrested, and fights killed two strikers and two alliance members and injured more than 60 people.

In August, the Teamsters won a union election, giving them what many feel was labor's first important victory in the state. Other union clashes followed the truckers battle, and in most instances, the victories went to the labor movement. One of the most _ significant was the organization attempt by the International Brotherhood of Electrical Workers at Northern States Power Co. in Minneapolis. A mass meeting of NSP employees was held on Feb. 23, 1937, protesting working conditions, safety standards, wages, holidays and overtime, seniority and other issues. The following day about 700 workers struck NSP, and a bitter fight followed. Union employees went throughout Minneapolis, opening switches and pulling fuses on power poles faster than company officials could prowl the alleys and find the trouble spots. More than 1,800 homes were without power at times. Strikers also put a 100,000-volt line out of service by sawing down the wood superstructure. Other transmission lines were shorted when strikers threw metal chains over them. After eight days of vandalism, the two sides got together and agreed on a settlement, including a promise that NSP would officially recommend to its workers that joining the union was in the best interest of both labor and management.

The unrest caused by the depression wasn't limited to labor strife. Minnesota underwent a political revolution as well. When Franklin Roosevelt easily defeated Herbert Hoover in the 1932 election, he became the first Democrat in Minnesota's history to carry the state for the nation's highest office. Governor Olson, representing the Farmer-Labor Party, had a difficult time controlling the demands of his followers. In 1934, The Farmer-Labor Party adopted a platform demanding state operation of all utilities, banks, mines, the state's transportation system and even factories. The governor and his state committee later amended the platform to remove most of those demands, but the feeling in the state that a government should take over much of private business was definitely growing.

The expanding role of government in the lives of all American citizens took a giant step during the 1930s as the public leaned more and more away from private enterprise. The leadership of President Roosevelt in that direction was a major factor. Dozens of laws were passed, both on the federal and state level, to give government a bigger voice in the affairs of the country. It was in the 1930s that the banking laws were overhauled; the rules governing stock market transactions were stiffened through the Securities Exchange Act; the Social Security program was enacted, and in Minnesota, the first state income tax was passed in 1933. Doing business in the future would never be as simple as it had been prior to the Great Depression.

Surprisingly, individual companies in Minnesota weathered the decade-long depression better than firms in most other states, possibly because of the traditionally conservative practices and strong leadership in the major companies. Minneapolis-Honeywell, for instance, bounced back quickly by finding new items to produce after sales of their regulators fell off drastically. The firm's annual revenues had plunged from $5.5 million in 1931 to only $3.5 million the following year, and the number of employees was reduced from 1,150 to 647. Production lines were shut down and machines stood idle. The company almost immediately began looking for new lines to manufacture. An arrangement was made with the Pillsbury Co. for Minneapolis-Honeywell to produce flour sifters as a premium to boost Pillsbury's sagging flour sales. More than two million sifters were manufactured by Minneapolis-Honeywell, activating several production lines. The company expanded its production of replacement gear trains for water meters, which it had been making as a specialty item for the Minneapolis Water Department. Other cities were contacted, and the line was greatly expanded. Sales increased to $4.5 million in 1933, and the number of employees increased to 1,197.

Honeywell purchased Brown Instrument Co. of Philadelphia in 1934, a decision that helped pull both firms out of the Depression doldrums. Brown, a company founded in 1859, manufactured recording, indicating and controlling instruments. Its annual sales were $1,624,920 the year it joined the Minneapolis corporation. Honeywell already was making valves and other accessories to complete the instruments started by Brown, so the merger of the two companies provided a neat fit. As a result of the acquisition and other moves to expand, Honeywell was well out of its slump by the end of 1934, and within two years, its sales had climbed to $13.5 million, and its payroll grew to 3,300, making it one of the few Minnesota firms to actually hire large number of new workers during the Depression.

There's no question that one of the major reasons businesses in Minnesota suffered less than those in other states from the ravages of the Great Depression was the relative stability of the banking system in the state, a situation due primarily to the formation of two large bank-holding companies a few months prior to the stock market collapse. The Northwest Bancorporation, with headquarters in Minneapolis, was formed in February 1929, and a few months later, the First Bank Stock Corp., put together by the First

National Banks of St. Paul and Minneapolis, began business. Both holding companies were formed in attempts to strengthen the weak banking system in the Ninth Federal Reserve District, a weakness caused, not by the Depression, but by the pitiful agricultural conditions in tfe region during the 1920s. Farmers in Minnesota and adjoining states were in the midst of their own economic crash for several years before the stock market collapsed. A long period of drought, rising land prices and sharp increases in taxes were pressing farmers all during the 1920s and caused an unusually large number of mortgage defaults. Rural banks especially felt the deteriorating agricultural situation, and, unable to collect on many farm loans, they had no choice but to close. During the 1920s, there were 2,333 bank failures in Minnesota and the states adjoining it. Most of them were country banks. Although not commonly known, there were more bank failures in this region during the so-called Roaring 20s than during the Depression decade of the 1930s.

Banking leaders in Minneapolis and St. Paul, the region's financial center, were worried about economic conditions a full year before the 1929 crash, and, fortunately, were taking some drastic action. Not only were they facing a severe rural banking crisis, but large eastern banks were making moves into the area with the intention of taking control of the weakened system. The first to act against this double threat was J. Cameron Thomson, an official with Northwestern National Bank of Minneapolis. Thomson warned that if something wasn't done immediately it would be the beginning of the end for the Twin Cities banking community. He convinced Northwestern's president, Edward W. Decker, to form a bank-holding company, which would give unity to the troubled rural banks and strengthen the hand of Northwestern against the invading eastern interests. In a history of Northwest Bancorporation, Harold Chucker, a Minneapolis economics writer, explains the strategy:

"The concept that was settled upon was a form of group banking. Based on the idea that in union there is strength, group banking seemed to offer advantages to the large city banks, as well as to the hard-pressed rural institutions. Above all, it promised to bring stability to what was rapidly becoming a chaotic situation. Under the group banking, or holding company, concept, each member bank was to retain its unit structure and continue to operate on a local basis, with its own board of directors. The parent organization—the bank holding company—was to provide specialized services of a better quality than affiliated banks could provide for themselves. The holding company was to sell stock to the public, with the proceeds used to help protect affiliated banks from adverse economic conditions. Shares of the individual banks would be exchanged for shares in the holding company."

Thomson was named general manager of the new holding company. In its first year of operation, Northwest Banco acquired 90 banks in the region, and by 1931 it had the majority interest in 127 banks. Meanwhile, the First Bank Stock Corp. was also taking shape, with Paul Leeman, George Prince and Clive Jaffray the three founding officers. This holding company, later to change its name to the First Bank System, used the same concept employed by Northwest Banco, and it operated in roughly the same territory. During the first four years of the Depression, the First channeled more than $8 million into its affiliated banks to keep them from closing.

And while thousands of banks around the country failed during the early years of the Depression, not a single affiliate of either holding company closed its doors. In fact, it was a period of considerable growth for some of the banks, especially the First National of St. Paul, which had merged with the Merchants National Bank early in 1929. To handle this expansion, the St. Paul bank constructed its present 32-story skyscraper at the corner of Fourth and Minnesota streets, completing the 402-foot structure in 1931 at a cost of $6,325,000.

The success of the holding companies while other businesses were suffering made Minnesota's Farmer-Labor governor, Floyd B. Olson, suspicious that something was crooked. He pressed the legislature to examine Northwest Banco's structure, but he was rebuffed, so the governor ordered the state Securities Commission to launch an investigation. A Hennepin County grand jury conducted a thorough investigation, but refused to return an indictment. Undaunted, Governor Olson then forced a lengthy trial against the officers of Northwest Banco at Moorhead, but it ultimately ended in favor of the bank holding company. The governor's over-zealous campaign against Northwest Banco, in effect, backfired on his party's attempt to blacken the image of Minnesota's free enterprise during the 1930s. Ralph Budd, who was president of Great Northern Railroad in St. Paul, during the Depression, summed up the feeling of many in the region when he said in 1939 that if it hadn't been for the stabilizing influence of the two bank holding companies "there would not have been a single bank open from Minneapolis to Seattle" during the depths of the Depression.

The stability of the banking system, especially in the Twin Cities, reflected on many other businesses throughout the Depression, and although there was a large number of failures among the marginal companies, nearly all of the major firms survived.

Nonetheless, it took unusual efforts to stay ahead of the worsening conditions as the decade progressed. While everyone kept looking for better days, the sharper businessmen prepared for a long period of austerity. George Draper Dayton, the founder of Dayton's Department Store in downtown Minneapolis and a leader of the state's business community, was leaned on heavily for advice, not only by local peers, but also by national leaders. He served as an unofficial adviser to President Herbert Hoover and his Reconstruction Finance Corp., formed in 1932 to help stimulate business. At a meeting in Washington, D.C., with most bureaucrats in attendance speaking of brighter days right around the corner, Dayton got up to admonish the optimists. He argued forcefully that conditions brought on by the Depression were *not* improving, and that its effects were spreading gradually into parts of the country that had been spared at the start. After the meeting, President Hoover asked Dayton to stay behind. "I want to thank you for your statement," Hoover said. "These other people have been telling me what they think I want to hear. Today, you have told me what I needed to know."

Dayton was referring to Minnesota when he said the Depression in 1932 was finally reaching areas not greatly affected earlier. His business, in fact, had the best year in its history in 1930, and the following year there was only a moderate falling off of sales. Dayton could see, however, that there wouldn't be a quick turnabout, and in 1932, he and his staff started a long-term campaign to bolster sagging revenues. For the remainder of the Depression, it was a rare occasion when there wasn't a sale of one type of another going on at the Dayton store. If it wasn't an Early Bird sale, it was an Anniversary sale, or Daisy Days, a Jubilee, Old Fashioned Bargain Days, Inventory sales—anything to get customers into the store. And as anyone who lived through the depression knows, there were bargains available everywhere. At Dayton's, you could buy men's shirts for 59 cents each, silk stockings at three pair for a dollar, raincoats for $1.79, women's shoes for $2.37 and top quality men's suits for $21. A three-piece bedroom suite in solid maple was on sale for $33.75.

The highly promotional Dayton's went through the entire Depression with a profit each year, and although annual sales were off, on the average, 28 percent compared to just before the Depression, most other department stores in the country saw sales drop by more than 50 percent in those money-tight days.

All in all, the years between 1930 and 1939 were probably the most trying to Minnesota business of any period in the history of the state, adversely affecting—to one degree or another—practically every company. Thousands of firms failed, and those that survived were mostly the well established organizations, and the majority of those experienced steeply declining sales, especially between 1932 and 1936.

One important lesson was learned by all businesspeople during the Depression: When times get tough, the outlook gloomy and you're absolutely convinced things can't get worse, they really can. The Depression also proved one other important fact: A well managed, fiscally strong company can survive just about any economic crisis.

Chapter 10

The contrast in business conditions in Minnesota between the Depression years of the 1930s and the war years of the 1940s borders on the unbelievable. The huge surplus of labor was suddenly replaced by a severe shortage, and stealing of workers became commonplace. In the 1930s, mountains of raw materials, machinery and equipment were available, but businesses couldn't afford them. In the 1940s, shortages of practically everything but money caused nightmares for managers. What makes the stark transition so remarkable is the speed with which it occurred. When war clouds over Europe and the Orient started drifting in the direction of the United States in the late 1930s, the depression here was still on. When World War II was finally brought directly to the United States by the Pearl Harbor attack on Dec. 7, 1941, the country's businesses had already begun the biggest production boom ever experienced.

Companies in Minnesota made the switch from peacetime activities to frenzied wartime production almost overnight. Literally thousands of corporations in the state were involved directly in the war effort, and those that weren't felt its immense effects. Practically every commercial enterprise experienced severe problems in finding and keeping employees. More than 300,000 Minnesotans left their jobs during the early 1940s to join the military services, and thousands of others traveled to Alaska, Greenland and the West Coast for higher paying defense jobs. Manufacturing plants in Minnesota doubled, tripled and quadrupled their capacities in a few short months, looking for help wherever they could find it and scrounging for equipment and building supplies. Wages and other costs soared. Compared to the problems of the Depression, however, these headaches for Minnesota businesses were a welcome change, and for most, the improving profit picture made the new challenges worthwhile.

Although the Japanese attack on Pearl Harbor was unexpected, American involvement in World War II wasn't, and preparations for an all-out conflict had been started many months before Congress officially declared war. And Minnesota, because of its large number of manufacturing concerns and, even more importantly, because of its relatively safe geographic location, became a prime supplier of military goods. Both the heavily industrialized East Coast and the populous West Coast were regarded by military leaders as the first targets for an enemy invasion and as reachable areas for bombing from the air.

The government looked inland for a relatively safe area to manufacture guns, ammunition and other goods for the war, and Minnesota businesses were involved early in this carefully planned strategy. A full month before war was declared, Minnesota companies had been awarded $346 million in contracts to produce military items. Those contracts were to exceed billions of dollars before the war ended.

Typical of this switch from normal peacetime manufacturing to war production was the situation at Owatonna Tool Co., a small plant in a small community in southern Minnesota. In 1939, the firm had 48 employees on one shift, manufacturing a line of tools for various purposes. Within months, because of military orders, the firm had more than 150 workers on three shifts seven days a week and still couldn't keep up with the ever increasing demand.

As the near certainty of an all-out war became generally accepted, companies through the state began switching their production to the defense effort, and many new firms were started. Several were financed and equipped by the federal government. Practically every major corporation was involved in some facet of war production. Minneapolis-Honeywell, already one of the leading manufacturers of instrument controls, began producing precision military equipment, such as airplane controls, and later expanded their lines of war goods even to include bombs. General Mills, Pillsbury and the other food companies were awarded contracts to supply food to the rapidly growing military services, and some of them diversified into totally unrelated lines. As an example, General Mills manufactured gun sights and torpedoes. Minnesota Mining and Manufacturing produced millions of feet of tape for the armed forces and defense plants in addition to making a variety of other war goods.

Munsingwear switched from making clothing for the civilian population to producing military garments, and a host of smaller clothing manfuacturers in the Twin Cities enlarged their work forces to sew uniforms for the military, which rapidly involved millions of men and women. Minneapolis Moline Power Implement Co. and the St. Paul branch of International Harvester converted from farm equipment to become two of the country's largest producers of armaments. The Ford Motor Co. assembly plant in St. Paul began to build military vehicles. The Seeger Refrigerator Co. in St. Paul started producing ammunition, and the Crown Iron Works Co. enlarged its Minneapolis facilities to build portable bridges and pontoons. American Hoist & Derrick of St. Paul manufactured winches and other equipment for the armed services and for the mushrooming defense plants across the country. The Minnesota Onan Corp. produced thousands of portable electric power plants and other types of generators. The Andersen Corp. at Bayport, using wood products from Northern Minnesota, built prefabricated huts that the Army Air Corps used around the world. The Flour City Ornamental Iron Co. in Minneapolis switched from ornate railings for homes to 54 different military items.

Dozens of huge new defense plants sprung up throughout Minnesota, and as large as they became, they still needed to subcontract much of their work to hundreds of small businesses throughout the state. Seven large shipbuilding yards in the Duluth-Superior area had more than $100 million in Navy contracts by mid-1942, and Cargill, Inc., of Minneapolis opened a large shipbuilding division at Savage to build tankers for the Navy. The Northwest Aeronautical Corp. in St. Paul began building gliders and fuel tanks for military airplanes.

The federal government was so convinced Minnesota offered a safe territory for defense plants and had such an exceptional record of productivity, that it spent millions of dollars on buildings and equipment here. The sprawling Twin City Ordnance Plant at new Brighton, managed by the Federal Cartridge Co., was actually a government-owned-and-operated facility during the war years, producing ammunition 24 hours a day, seven days a week.

By far the best example of Minnesota's rapid conversion trom peacetime operations to frenetic wartime production is the startling story behind the Northern Pump Co., and its energetic chief executive, John Blackstock Hawley Jr. Hawley joined the Twin Cities company as an engineer in 1924 at the age of 23 when Northern Pump had a total workforce of 50 workers, making pumps for fire engines. Before World War II ended, Hawley was in charge of a $20-million plant in Fridley with nearly 15,000 employees working every hour of every day making guns for the Navy. Northern Pump Co., later to be called Northern Ordnance, was the Navy's largest ordnance producer during the war, and in the early 1940s, it was the largest defense plant in the country that had started from scratch. A gun made by Northern Pump fired the first shot against the enemy, sinking a Japanese submarine near Pearl Harbor on Dec. 7, 1941.

The incredible Northern Pump story starts back in 1907 with the formation of the Northern Fire Apparatus Co. in Minneapolis. The firm manufactured light fire-fighting equipment for hand-drawn vehicles and later started building equipment for horse-drawn and then motorized fire engines. A Twin Cities machinist, Theodore Pagel, meanwhile, was inventing a rotary pump to be used on fire engines, and in 1910, his company, Pagel Pump, was merged with the Northern Fire Apparatus Co. into Northern Pump.

John B. Hawley Jr., a graduate of Cornell University, had just been discharged from a tuberculosis sanitarium when he joined Northern Pump. His real love was inventing things. He had already sold one invention for $27,000 and by 1928, had invented an improved pump which he sold to Northern Pump in exchange for controlling interest in the company. Hawley worked on a percentage of his firm's profits, and during the Depression, as he later recalled, he earned hardly enough as the owner of the firm to pay his personal expenses. By 1939, however, Northern Pump had turned the corner. It was producing equipment not for fire departments and had landed its first contract with the U.S. Navy. The Navy was impressed with Hawley's methods. Using pumps on board ships that weighed as much as 1,800 pounds, the Navy had asked Hawley and his firm to design a comparable model that weighed less. Hawley came up with a submersible pump that weighed only 98 pounds but had twice the pumping capacity of the heavier units.

So, when the Navy decided in 1940 it needed a plant located in a safe, secure place to build gun mounts for its ships, it looked toward Minnesota and, naturally, to Jack Hawley. He remembers that in early fall, 1940, "Washington simply called us to hop on a $5-million, new-plant job right away, and we hopped."

Hawley said the Navy told him it would like to have the plans for the new plant in about 90 days. "Hell," I told them, "I'll have the plant built and in operation before then." And he did. Drawing up his own plans and specifications, Hawley selected a 350-acre cow pasture in Fridley near the Minneapolis filtration plant and immediately began construction. Starting in the first week of October 1940, Hawley had the site leveled within a couple of days, and a week later, the foundations for the first of five buildings were already laid. By the end of October, more than half of the main 1,200-foot-long building had been erected. About 500 construction workers were working around-the-clock, seven days a week on the complex. The rapid progress amazed experienced contractors in the area, to say nothing of the astounded Navy officials. Hawley's crews kept up their pace even during one of the worst blizzards in Minnesota's history in November 1940, working and sleeping on continuous rotating four-hour shifts, day and night, with 70-mile-an-hour winds blowing the 16 inches of new snow through the partly completed buildings while temperatures dipped to zero and below.

By January 1941, the five huge buildings were completed, and $3 million worth of precision equipment was moved from Northern Pump's old plant in Minneapolis on a 10-mile railroad built between it and the new facility. Because of the military nature of the new business, the move was made in secrecy under heavy guard. Work on the Navy gun contract had already started at the old plant, and the move caused only a half-day delay in production. By mid-1941 Hawley had more than $100 million in Navy contracts to construct gun mounts and hydraulic equipment. He had more than 4,000 skilled workers on the job before the new complex was a year old, becoming the largest employer in Minnesota almost overnight. Before World War II directly involved the United States, Hawley's new facility had six large buildings, consisting of an administration office, four assembly plants, each a quarter-of-a-mile long, plus a 150-by-1,300-foot warehouse, holding rough castings and pigs of aluminum, bronze and other metals used in his own foundry. In the main plants, there were millions of dollars in new equipment, including a mammoth 500-ton press that could straighten out sheets of two-inch-thick steel plates to an accuracy of a thousandth of an inch.

Hawley's men were working as many hours as they wanted, with many putting in 72 hours a week on a regular basis. With labor getting extremely short, Hawley was accused by other businessmen in the state of stealing their skilled workmen. By late 1942, Northern Pump had 7,000 workers and appeared to have little trouble finding qualified help. Major employers in the state held a meeting to discuss the labor shortage, and speaker after speaker got up to express the hope that no firm would resort to pirating, or "scamping" as the practice of stealing workers was called. It was agreed, then, that this practice was to be condemned. The business leaders then called upon Hawley to hear his views.

"I assume you invited me here because I am stealing your

workers," Hawley said. "I am paying a ten-dollar bonus to any man in my plant for each good man he can persuade to come to work for me. About overtime, my men work till they drop. They come out of the plant all bent over; they can hardly stagger to the gate. But one peek at their pay check and they all feel swell. Sure, I'm stealing men. I've got to have them. This is Navy work. But I'll tell you what, you fellows appoint a committee, tell me what I ought to do, and I'll abide by any plan you think up." The committee's main suggestions were that Hawley encourage the men to work even more overtime to reduce the total work force he'd need, and to pay a $20 bonus, so his own men might try to attract workers from plants farther away from the state.

Hawley used every scheme imaginable to keep his workers on the job as long as possible. In addition to overtime pay, he'd give $1,250 in door prizes every weekend to sweeten those less desirable shifts. There was free coffee available at all times, and meals were served from "rolling kitchens" to the men at their posts. The food wasn't free, but it was sold at prices below Hawley's cost. The workers, who even had their autos serviced free of charge while they were on the jobs, were kings during those trying war days.

Hawley himself worked 20-hour days, sometimes not leaving the plant for days at a time, keeping himself going with light snacks and liberal doses of Scotch. He continually amazed Navy officials by beating production schedules with ease. By late 1943, he was a full two years ahead of the schedule originally laid down by the Navy. When Hawley got his first Navy order for 5-inch anti-aircraft mounts, he plastered signs throughout the sprawling plant which read, "Blitz 100!" That meant he wanted 100 gun mounts completed by Christmas, a self-imposed deadline the Navy thought was impossible to meet. By Dec. 4, 1941, however, three days before Pearl Harbor and 21 days before his own impossible deadline, Hawley had the 100 guns ready to ship. The 100th one was painted red, white and blue, and production was stopped for everyone to let out a cheer and to hear Hawley say he was increasing everyone's pay. But then it was back to work.

Gun mounts produced at Northern Pump included every part of the finished weapon except the barrel. Parts were made at Hawley's plant and in 55 other foundries in the region. The guns were superior to anything produced anywhere in the world, according to proud Navy officials. They called the Northern Pump facility "the finest machine shop on the globe." Each gun mount contained from 15 to 39 tons of high-precision machinery, and they were designed so they could swing bolt upright to shoot at high-flying enemy bombers, and then suddenly swing downward to fire a shell 15 miles across the water.

Hawley himself, having designed and built much of it personally, was able to operate most of the complicated machinery in the plant. He was impressed with machinery. When praised for his rapid completion of the buildings at the Fridley plant, Hawley scoffed at the accomplishment. "It doesn't take any brains to put up a static structure," he said. "To build something dymanic—a variable-pitch propellor or a magneto—that's what takes brains. There is more brainwork in one magneto than in all the buildings in the U.S."

Hawley was intolerant with bureaucratic red tape, and was not a popular figure with many government officials in Washington. He had a sign posted at his plant that read: "We must become intolerant of delay. We must tear our way through red tape. We must pillory bureaucrats who stupidly sacrifice time in the pursuit of an impossible perfection." Hawley often went ahead with orders before receiving final approval on test models, seriously jeopardizing his own profit situation. If a contract had been rejected, he could have been stuck with equipment that couldn't be sold. As sole owner of this company, however, with no stockholders or investors to consult, Hawley often went blindly ahead in production, risking millions of dollars on his confidence that his prototypes would be accepted.

And although he personally made many millions during the war years, he was constantly borrowing money to keep his huge complex expanding, and was deeply in debt throughout those years. "When I was 28," he said, recalling the sale of his first invention, "I had money. During the war years I must have owed 15 to 20 million dollars most of the time. That was my life—a sort of cumulative bankruptcy." By his own admission in late 1943, Hawley said he had made more than $40 million, but that was before taxes, which were exceptionally steep during the war years. In 1942, when President Roosevelt recommended that top salaries for U.S. civilians should be limited to $25,000 a year during the duration of the war, Hawley voluntarily cut his pay, which had been $448,000 the year before, to the $25,000 figure. Hawley wrote to the President, saying, "your recent recommendation that salaries should be limited to $25,000 per year after taxes in the best interest of the war effort is reasonable." Apparently Hawley didn't lose much take-home pay, however. Federal income taxes in 1943 would have taken about $340,000 of Hawley's $448,000 salary, and state income taxes would have taken another $40,000.

Hawley's equity in the enormous plant was growing each year, and because his financial affairs have always been kept very private, his actual net worth has never been revealed.

Hawley sold the Fridley plant to FMC Corp. in 1964, and it is still producing weapons for the military as the Northern Ordnance Division of FMC. Northern Pump Co., which had been the holding company before the sale to FMC, is still owned by Hawley. Today it is primarily engaged in oil properties, real estate and a 3,000-acre farm near McHenry, IL, approximately 55 miles from the Chicago loop.

To commemorate Hawley's contribution to the war effort, his company received six Navy E awards for outstanding performance. Hawley personally received from the Navy its highest distinguished service medal awarded to civilians.

The period between 1940 and the end of World War II in 1945 will go down as one of the most exciting times for Minnesota business, but it was a period which everyone knew would end, and the transition back to peacetime operations would probably be just as traumatic as the switch to wartime production. And it was.

Chapter 11

The end of World War II in 1945 caused a great amount of turmoil for Minnesota manufacturers engaged in defense work. They knew that when the war ended, the demand for their products would evaporate overnight, and although they expected it, the executives operating these plants were so busy producing war goods right up to the time of the Japanese surrender, they had little time to prepare for the inevitable falloff of orders.

When the war ended, many of them were practically walking around in a daze, wondering what the future held for them. Typical of these bewildered businessmen was John E. Parker, founder and the chief executive of Northwestern Aeronautical Corp. (NAC) of St. Paul. NAC operated a government-owned facility at 1902 Minnehaha Ave. in St. Paul, building wooden gliders for the Army Air Corps and fuel tanks for military aircraft.

A Washington, D.C. resident before the war, Parker was a graduate of the Annapolis Naval Academy and had embarked on a career as an investment banker before the war started. When the military officials in Washington decided on the need for a glider-manufacturing facility, they selected Parker to head the project and Minnesota as the site for the huge factory. Parker and NAC built more than 1,500 gliders before the war ended, including those used in the Normandy invasion in 1944. The wooden craft were military personnel carriers used in airborne assaults.

One of the larger defense plants in Minnesota, and the second largest glider-manufacturer in the country during the war, NAC found itself without a single order shortly after the war ended. Founded specifically for the war effort, NAC had no peacetime product and no experience in any other field. Parker enjoyed living in Minnesota, still had his manufacturing facility, and wanted to continue in business here. All he needed was a product.

While Parker was looking, another displaced veteran of the war effort was trying to interest someone with money in an idea he had. This was William C. Norris, a Nebraska native who found himself at the end of the war a lieutenant commander in the Navy working on secret cryptographic analysis for a hush-hush military agency in Washington. A 1932 graduate of the University of Nebraska, Norris was an electrical engineer working for

Westinghouse when the war began. His experience with the Navy excited Norris about the future possibilities of experiments in the new field of electronics he had been conducting, and his idea was to establish a business to design and fabricate equipment for a market he knew existed in the government.

The field of electronic computers was in its infancy in 1945, but Norris, who later founded Control Data Corp., now one of the giants in the computer industry, was convinced there was an entirely new world opening up in this direction. Norris was on the ground floor of the exciting computer age, and unlike others who joined him, clearly saw the vast opportunities ahead. An associate of Norris, who observed his uncanny ability throughout the years, said, "Bill Norris can see further into the future than any man I've ever met."

In 1945, however, Norris was having trouble finding people to accept his vision, especially someone with the capital to back his idea. Norris did convince two other Navy veterans, Howard T. Engstrom and Ralph L. Meader, of the merits of his plan, but, like Norris, they had skills in computer technology, but lacked the one essential ingredient—money. Engstrom had worked in Washington with Norris in projects on equipment for deciphering secret codes and on punched-card devices which were the predecessors of today's computers. Meader, a Navy captain, was in charge of the Navy's Computing Machines Laboratory at a military department inside the National Cash Register Co. in Dayton, Ohio. Meader had planned to stay on with National Cash Register after the Navy had requested the company to continue in computer work after the war. The company, in what turned out to be a blunder, rejected the offer in preference to devoting its energies to producing cash registers. The company later got into the computer business, but never caught up to the firms who were first in the field.

Norris, Engstrom and Meader were now firmly agreed they could start a computer company if they could find financial backing. They easily convinced a large group of restless military veterans, each highly qualified with engineering or other technical backgrounds, to join their project. The months slipped by, however, without an actual company being formed, and the three founders began to worry their skilled team of experts would find other opportunities before they could get started.

Then, in late 1945, Meader was introduced to the Northwestern Aeronautical Corp. founder, John Parker, through a mutual friend at the National Cash Register Co. facility in Dayton, Ohio. Parker, still looking for a worthwhile product for his empty St. Paul facility, immediately was interested in Meader's plan. Parker then met with Norris and Engstrom, who provided further details. Before Parker would commit himself, however, he arranged a meeting with top Navy officials in Washington where Meader, Norris and Engstrom could fully explain the nature of their proposed business. The senior Navy officers present listened with interest, and said if the group formed a company, it could count on some immediate government contracts in the computer exploration field.

Parker was convinced. He arranged the financing and turned over the NAC facility in St. Paul to the new firm. On Jan. 8, 1946, Engineering Research Associates (ERA) was incorporated in Minnesota with half-ownership going to Parker and the investors he had lined up, and the other half to Meader, Norris, Engstrom and their crew. The initial investment was only $20,000, but Parker agreed to put up another $200,000 as it was needed. Parker was named ERA president with Meader, Norris and Engstrom each appointed a vice president.

With the 40 technical men Norris had already recruited, ERA was in business immediately. Other engineers and scientists, out of work after duty in either the military or defense plants, eagerly applied for jobs at ERA. Each new employee was required to buy some stock in the new company. Two Navy contracts were received as promised, and work got under way.

The company's plant at 1902 Minnehaha Ave. was far from being ideally suited for work by skilled professionals on electronic experiments. It was originally a foundry for the American Radiator Co., then a warehouse used by the government during the depression, and finally a glider-manufacturing plant during the war. The building had high ceilings with skylights which opened and closed by pulleys, but they operated very slowly, and when it rained the scientists and engineers could expect to get drenched before the skylights were closed. And there were usually more birds in the building than workers, except in the winter when the birds left for warmer climates. The ERA staff coped with cold working conditions by wearing coats and mittens at their drawing boards.

In August 1947, ERA received a contract to design and build the first general purpose computer system. It was completed in late 1950 and installed in a National Security Agency facility in

Washington, D.C. The system, called the Atlas, was the first step in the new, booming computer age. Another Atlas was delivered to the same agency in 1953, and a year later, a modified version, called the ERA 1101, was designed and built for commercial use. The world's first commercial computer was a giant, weighing more than 16,000 pounds. The ERA 1101 consisted of seven cabinets, occupying a space 45 feet long by nine feet wide, housing 2,700 vacuum tubes and miles of electrical wiring.

While this first computer was being constructed, other, more advanced models were being designed at the ERA plant, which had more than 700 employees testing and building various electronic systems.

Because ERA was one of the first computer companies in the United States, other firms, as they entered the field, looked to the skilled technicians at the St. Paul facility for trained workmen. Among those successfully recruiting some top ERA staff was Remington Rand, Inc., which entered the computer field in 1949. Remington Rand enlarged its operations in 1950 when it acquired Eckert Mauchly Computer Corp., and on Dec. 6, 1951, it offered the shareholders of ERA a tidy $1.5 million for ownership of the Minnesota company. The acquisition wasbcompleted a few months later, and the original shareholders of ERA each received a sum 80 times what they had invested in 1946.

Interestingly, in buying ERA, Remington Rand, got more than it had bargained for. ERA, under a top secret government contract, was working on an advanced computer, to be called the Atlas II, which could not be disclosed to Remington Rand officials, because they did not have the proper security classifications. It was after the purchase was completed before the company's top executives even knew of the existence of the vastly superior Atlas II model. The Atlas II, also called the ERA 1103, was a whopping success for the new owners. Four systems were sold in 1953, and 16 others eventually were marketed before even better models were introduced.

Remington Rand, with its Minnesota-based ERA facility, its Eckert Mauchly Computer Co. subsidiary in Philadephia, and its own computer development laboratories in Norwalk, Conn., was clearly the dominant computer company in the world. With a decided advantage in the manufacturing area, Remington Rand decided in 1953 to strengthen its sales and marketing program by opening a consolidated selling office in New York. The ERA president, John Parker, was moved to New York to head the office.

Parker was instrumental in keeping Remington Rand far ahead of the nearest competitor, International Business Machines (IBM), during the mid-1950s. Parker beat out IBM with several significant computer sales to such firms as U.S. Steel, Metropolitan Life Insurance Co., General Electric and Westinghouse.

As Remington Rand's computer operations began to mushroom, however, its needs for expansion capital was becoming critical, mainly due to the fact its computers were being rented instead of sold. With so much of its energies now being devoted to financial problems, Remington Rand began to lose ground quickly to the aggressive and fiscally healthier IBM.

James Rand, the head of Remington Rand, decided the only solution was to sell his company to a heavily capitalized firm, so on June 30, 1955, his firm was sold to Sperry Gyroscope Co., and the new Sperry Rand Corp. resulted. One of the first steps taken by the new owners was to consolidate all the various computer arms into a single division, and the head of ERA in St. Paul, William Norris, was named general manager of all computer operations, to be called the Univac Division of Sperry Rand.

The Univac Division, which eventually grew to a volume exceeding $2 billion annually in revenues with more than 50,000 employees worldwide, still has its main manufacturing facilities in Minnesota and in the late 1970s had more than 12,000 workers in several Twin Cities plants.

Norris managed the vast computer operations for Sperry Rand for the next two years, and although 80 percent of all computers in service in the U.S. came from his division, he could see the ambitious IBM making rapid strides that worried him more than his Sperry Rand superiors. He also realized that future sales of computers would be in the commercial area and not so dependent on government use, as had been the case. Norris felt a frontal attack by Sperry Rand against IBM would be prohibitively expensive.

In 1957, Norris made a decision. He would form his own computer manufacturing company in Minnesota, and instead of competing head-on against IBM and Sperry Rand, he would specialize in computer equipment they didn't offer. He had much quicker success in finding financial support with his new firm, Control Data Corp., than he experienced in forming ERA. Within 10 days of issuing a mimeographed prospectus, Norris sold enough stock in a public offering to form his corporation. He had 300 stockholders buying 615,000 shares of common stock at $1 a share, enough to get started. Norris himself invested $75,000 in the new company. He opened offices in July 1957 on the second floor of the McGill Building, 501 Park Ave., in Minneapolis, across the street from the Minneapolis Star & Tribune Building. On Nov. 25 that year, Control Data purchased the Cedar Engineering Co., which had manufacturing facilities in St. Louis Park, a western Minneapolis suburb. Cedar, which had been making instruments and control devices, had $2 million in annual sales, 165 employees, and was acquired for $428,000.

There were problems galore in the early years for Norris and Control Data, and the situation appeared particularly glum when he and his top 20 executives all took 50 percent cuts in their salaries, and the company stock dropped to a low of 25 cents a share. Faith in his own ability and the extremely favorable investment conditions existing in those days in the stock market pulled Norris through the trying period. He said in 1957 that his personal goal for Control Data was $25 million in sales at the end of five years. By 1962, Control Data showed $42 million in sales with a half-million dollars profit. The stock had climbed to a high of $35 a share that year, after an earlier three-for-one split, which meant that the original stockholders had seen the value of each $1 share soar to $105 in less than five years.

Control Data had more than 2,000 employees in 1962, had moved its headquarters to the Minneapolis suburb of Bloomington, and had acquired two small computer companies, had opened data centers in other states, sales offices throughout the U.S. and in several foreign countries, and, most importantly, was working on the world's largest and most powerful computer.

In 1963, the year Control Data stock was listed on the New York Stock Exchange, the company introduced its giant computer, the CDC 6600, a machine which staggered the industry. Containing 350,000 transistors and resistors and 80 miles of electrical wiring, the 6600 was the undisputed king of computers. This had been Norris' strategy from the beginning—to build computers not offered by IBM, Sperry Rand or other competitors. And while he was not competing with them, they weren't happy with the upstart Norris and his young Control Data organization.

T.J. Watson Jr ., head of IBM, by then the leader in the computer industry, wrote a memo, dated Aug. 28, 1963, which clearly expressed his feelings about Norris and Control Data. The memo, sent to Watson's seven top assistants, read:

"Last week, Control Data had a press conference during which they officially announced their 6600 system. I understand that in the laboratory developing this system, there are only 34 people, including the janitor. Of these, 14 are engineers and four are programmers, and only one person had a Ph.D., a relatively junior programmer. To the outsider, the laboratory appeared to be cost conscious, hard working and highly motivated. Contrasting this modest effort with our vast development activities, I fail to understand why we have lost our industry leadership position by letting someone else offer the world's most powerful computer. I think top priority should be given to discussion as to what we are doing wrong and how we should go about changing it immediately.''

From that point on, even though Norris wasn't interested in competing with IBM, Watson saw to it that IBM competed with Control Data.

Norris, with the help of unusually healthy activity in Control Data stock trading, embarked on an aggressive acquisition program during the mid-1960s, greatly expanding the company's operations and production capabilities. Starting in early 1963 with the acquisition of the computer division of the Bendix Corp., Control Data went on to buy Meiscon Co., a civil engineering firm; Electrofact of Holland, which gave the firm an entry into the common market; Digraphics Division of Itek; Bridge, Inc., a manufacturer of peripheral products; Rabinow Engineering; OCR Systems; the Transactor Division of Stromberg; Adcomp; Data Display; Datatrol; Computec; Preston Associates; Librascope Division of General Precision; Howard Research, and Waltec Ltd. of Hong Kong.

Norris was serving notice on the entire computer industry that his Minnesota company would be a serious contender in what was becoming a highly competitive field.

IBM, however, was carefully planning its own strategy against Control Data, and its proposed entry into the giant computer business almost destroyed Norris' organization by 1966. IBM, shortly after Watson's memo about Control Data, announced with great fanfare its 360 computer, a system which it said would perform both small and large computing chores, and then later its 360/90 system which was even bigger and better. The IBM announcements posed a serious problem for Control Data, because many potential customers decided to wait until the IBM systems were available, causing a sharp falloff of orders for Norris.

The active competition from IBM forced Control Data to cut its prices and to make several concessions to customers, such as penalty clauses. A good example was in the 1965 bidding for a large computer for the Bettis Atomic Power Laboratory, operated by Westinghouse. It needed a big system and accepted IBM's lower bid, but, then suspecting the proven capabilities of the Control Data 6600 would better answer its needs, asked Control Data to requote. Norris knocked down the price to $6 million and a 6600 was installed in September, with a penalty clause as part of the contract. Troubles developed after installation, and as Control Data technicians worked feverishly to correct them, the company was penalized $3,000 a day for 180 days until the system was running smoothly.

In addition to the stiff competition, Control Data was facing other serious problems as 1966 arrived. The leasing of machines was becoming more popular, causing a cash flow problem for Norris, and Control Data stock was falling, making it more difficult to obtain financing. The large number of acquisitions was causing a tremendous drain on capital, the company's research and development requirements had to grow in order to stay competitive, and as costs rose and sales fell, the company's profits dropped, further hurting the price of the stock.

Norris was faced with probably his most serious crisis in early 1966. It appeared he had three options: sell the company or parts of it, borrow enough money to stay alive, or borrow a large amount of money and continue to expand and compete with the industry giants.

Norris spent little time on the first two options and by February 1966 had talked 10 banks into setting up $120 million in a revolving credit account for Control Data. It was enough to pull the company out of the slump, and things began to pick up from this point. By the end of fiscal 1966, Control Data was able to show a profit of nearly $2 million on $167 million in sales. The company now had more than 11,000 employees. In July that year, Control Data had its biggest month in its history with $60 million in orders. The worst seemed over. By the end of fiscal 1967, the company had earned more than $14 million on $328 million in sales, and its stock was selling at nearly $80 a share after a three-for-two split the year before.

Perhaps the boldest move ever made by Norris, and one of his most successful achievements, was the acquisition of Commercial Credit Corporation in 1968. It seemed impossible that Control Data, with total assets of only $350 million, could expect to buy giant Commercial Credit, with assets of more than $3.5 billion, but Norris completed the purchase in June 1968 with $700 million in Control Data stock as the price. Commercial Credit, with headquarters in Maryland, was involved in consumer loans, leasing and insurance besides offering data processing services. It also had some manufacturing plants. In later years, when computer profits declined, it was the steady earnings from Commercial Credit which kept Control Data healthy and able to expand.

As the 1960s ended, Control Data was regarded in business circles throughout the country as a classic textbook example of what a brilliant entrepreneur could do with an idea. Norris in the dozen years since founding his company, had sales in 1969 of over a billion dollars with more than $41 million in profit. Control Data stock was trading at $160 a share, and the company had more than 40,000 employees throughout the world. The company started construction that year also on its new $15 million headquarters building in Bloomington.

The 1970s, with its recessions and other problems, caused setbacks for Control Data along with all businesses, but shrewd management by Norris and his assistants prevented any serious crises. The company topped the $2 billion in annual sales mark in 1976, and has joined the other Minnesota business giants as another good example of just how far a small concern can go.

Control Data, although the most successful, was only one of many Minnesota computer companies spinning off from the original ERA experiment in St. Paul.

Norris, Parker and the other scientists and technicians who were busy chasing birds out of the former glider plant in St. Paul during the late 1940s could have never dreamed that within 30 years they would have spawned not only the multi-billion dollar Control Data Corp., but more than two dozen other computer companies in Minnesota.

The ERA operation, in addition to providing the nucleus for today's giant Sperry Univac, was the training ground for future executives in nearly all the country's top electronics firms. In 1957, when Norris left ERA to form Control Data, three other companies evolved from ERA—Fabritek, Midwest Circuits and Transistor Electronics. The following year, Data Display, Inc., was organized by former ERA officials. General Magnetics started in 1959 as a brainchild of ERA staffers. In the 1960s, restless ERA executives left to form Comserv, Analysts International, Telex, Whitehall Electronics, Electro Med, Comten, Flo-Tronics, Nuclear Data, Data Management, Theratron, Minneapolis Scientific Controls, Aries Corp., Tronchemics Research, United Software and Community Electronics. Such Twin Cities-based companies as Data Card and Data 100 can trace their roots back to the ERA organization. And from the companies formed by that original group, other firms have split into a third generation, such as Cray Research.

In addition to Control Data and Univac, another major factor in the computer business today is Honeywell Inc. Honeywell entered the computer business in 1955 through a joint venture with Raytheon in a company called Datamatic. In 1970 the firm acquired the computer business of General Electric Corp which made Honeywell, at the time, second in size in the computer industry after IBM. Most of Honeywell's computer production facilities are located outside Minnesota in Massachusetts, Phoenix, Ariz., and Tampa and St. Petersburg, Fla. Even IBM, which from its Armon,, N.Y., headquarters, took away Minnesota's hope of being the computer capital of the world, eventually constructed a large computer facility at Rochester, Minn., employing about 5,000 highly skilled workers.

Because IBM decided to spread its computer plants throughout the world instead of concentrating them in one location, Minnesota today still is among the top states in computer production. Only California has more workers in the computer industry than Minnesota.

Of the world's top five computer manufacturers, four of them—IBM, Honeywell, Sperry Univac and Control Data—are either headquartered in Minnesota or have huge facilities here. There are more than 100 electronics-related firms based in Minnesota, with about 80 devoting most of their efforts to computers.

One of the more important aspects of the computer industry to Minnesota's business health is that it's an all-new category since World War II, and a badly needed replacement for the diminishing lumbering, flour milling and iron ore industries which built the state. The computer business is also a highly desirable industry in these days of worry about pollution and the drain on natural resources. It's a brain industry with a clean image, and it adds high quality people to the state's important work force.

As one industry executive says, "The computer industry has done more for Minnesota's self-image, in the quality of life area, than the Guthrie Theater and the Mayo Clinic put together."

Chapter 12

The significant birth of the computer industry to the Minnesota business family hasn't been the only child added since the end of World War II, and Control Data's brilliant leader, William Norris, hasn't been the only remarkable entrepreneur to shake up things in the state during the past 30 years.

There have been dozens of other new industries started here since the atomic bomb put a sudden end to the country's last big war—most notably, the medical products field—and there have been hundreds of capable business leaders adequately filling the shoes of those Minnesota giants previously discussed in this book.

Two of the state's present-day industrial titans almost certainly to be included in everyone's list of extraordinary business personalities are Curtis LeRoy Carlson, a Minneapolis-born wizard of Swedish ancestry, and Luigino Francesco Paulucci, better known as Jeno, the rambunctious son of an Italian-born iron ore miner in Hibbing, Minn.

Both men are the proud recipients of the national Horatio Alger award, the most fitting of all the honors bestowed on them. Each started his business career in Minnesota with absolutely nothing going for him except pluck and hard work, and each built multimillion-dollar corporate empires in rapid fashion.

Carlson, in fact, entered the magical billion-dollar category with his Twin Cities-based Carlson Companies in 1978, and has set his goal of reaching the two billion-dollar mark in annual sales in 1982. The portly, silver-haired Carlson, who was 64 in 1979, has collected an impressive string of more than 100 companies without ever having to sell a single share of stock to the public. His personal net worth, although never publicly disclosed, has been estimated at well in excess of $100 million.

In 1938, when Carlson was selling soap for Procter & Gamble Co. for less than $100 a month in salary, his prospects to become a multi-millionaire weren't so bright. A recent graduate of the University of Minnesota, Carlson took the job with Procter & Gamble over better paying opportunities, because it meant he could stay in Minnesota. His driving ambition, however, was to have a business himself, and he didn't wait long to get started.

Carlson became fascinated with the then-new idea of giving trading stamps to customers buying merchandise. One of the few businesses doing so was the Leader Department Store, located across from Powers in Minneapolis. It gave Security Red Stamps to all customers, and Carlson slyly bribed a secretary at the store with $10 to let him study the contract it had with the stamp company. The more he studied the more he felt he could improve on the entire stamp concept.

Completely without funds, Carlson talked his landlord into letting him postpone his $55 monthly rental payment so he could go into business for himself. He drew up his own incorporation papers, without the help of an attorney, and formed the Gold Bond Stamp Co. This was the humble beginning of the far-flung Carlson Companies empire, and like most new ventures, the first few years were painful. He slowly built up a network of stores using Gold Bond Stamps as an incentive to attract customers, and within a dozen years became a leader in this growing industry.

Carlson's first big coup came in 1952 when he convinced the Twin Cities-based Super Valu Food Stores chain to promote Gold Bond stamps in all its outlets. Super Valu was the first large group to give stamps to customers, but within 10 years every large food chain in the country, with the exception of A & P, was handling some type of trading stamps, and more than 70 percent of all the food sold in the U.S. was accompanied by stamps.

The astute Carlson could see that the stamp market was becoming saturated, and if he was to attain his growth goals, he would have to diversify. The decline in the popularity of trading stamps didn't occur until 1968, but by then Carlson was involved in other fields and safely protected from the doldrums affecting the stamp industry. In 1962 Carlson entered the hotel business by entering a partnership with the late Tom Moore, owner of the Radisson Hotel in downtown Minneapolis. Moore later sold his interest to Carlson, and since then the hotel phase of the Carlson Companies has grown to more than 20 complexes throughout the U.S. and in several foreign countries.

From hotels, Carlson further diversified into property development, business incentives other than stamps, food wholesaling, catalog showrooms, manufacturing and then boldly into the highly competitive restaurant business. Carlson's restaurant group now consists of two national chains, Country Kitchen, Inc., which operates and licenses more than 300 restaurants throughout the country, and TGI Friday's Restaurant, a smaller chain which is currently being expanded into more than 40 major cities in the U.S.

The Carlson Companies has recently entered the energy industry, the design and construction field, and optical equipment, and has its eyes on other areas. With more than 10,000 employees, the Carlson Companies, like Cargill, Inc., is one of the country's biggest private corporations.

Curt Carlson's business philosophy can be summed up in a statement he made several years ago to a reporter for the New York Times: "Almost any large diversified company starts with one little idea that works."

The "little idea" which started Jeno Paulucci on his road to being a multi-millionaire was the stubborn notion there was no reason why an Italian-American couldn't sell Chinese food in a Scandinavian state like Minnesota. Besides, he had firmly decided he didn't want to go down into the iron ore mines for 35 cents an hour as his father had. Jeno was going into the food business.

Paulucci started off selling fresh produce around Northeastern Minnesota, and his flair for aggressive salesmanship came naturally. Once, stuck with a load of bananas going brown, he peddled them quickly by touting them as "Argentina bananas," noted for their unusual coloring. Paulucci, who was 61 in 1979, started his Chun King Corp. in Duluth right after World War II with borrowed capital of $2,500. Arriving at work frequently as early as 4:30 a.m., Paulucci put in long days and nights to build his company into a national concern.

"I work hard," Jeno says. "I'm working holidays, Saturdays and Sundays. And I love every minute of it. Every day is exciting for me."

A day in November 1966 was one of Paulucci's most exciting. He sold his Chun King company to the tobacco giant, Reynolds Co., for $63 million in cash, and he became chairman of the Reynolds Food Division. "I was gung ho at first," Jeno recalls. "I wanted to go, go, go, but I soon found out that I was part of something much bigger than I was used to, something that I found almost impossible to move." Paulucci was headquartered in New York, and he simply didn't like it. He moved back to Minnesota and started to build a second empire.

Paulucci owned a smaller company, Northland Foods, which he didn't include in his sale to Reynolds, and he renamed it Jeno's, Inc., and was back into the food business in a big way—this time with pizza products and Italian snack foods. After losing $2 million during the first two years, Paulucci turned the company around in the third year, and it has been profitable ever since.

By 1979, Jeno's, a privately held company, was grossing approximately $150 million in annual sales and had about 2,000 employees at its headquarters in Duluth and at other facilities. Paulucci also is a major owner of Cornelius Co., a publicly held company based in the Twin Cities with annual revenues of more than $93 million.

Like most entrepreneurs, not everything Paulucci touched has turned to gold. He describes his venture into the mutual fund business as "one of my biggest blunders ever." He bought First Sierra Corp., based in San Francisco, with some of the proceeds of his Chun King sale, but the mutual fund business proved disappointing to him and it was sold a few years later. Paulucci also has tried the restaurant business, but isn't giving up. "Seven times I've gone on my own into fast foods and restaurants and seven times I've failed," Jeno told a Chicago Tribune reporter in 1978, "but I'll make it yet."

Paulucci has also entered the publishing business by starting a magazine in 1979 called Attenzione, a periodical aimed at Italian-Americans, which discusses the positives of Italy. This project is not designed so much as a money maker but an attempt "to repay my heritage." Paulucci's parents were both born in Blezwo Solfare in the Abruzzi mountains in Italy.

A longtime associate of Paulucci, in an interview with Corporate Report magazine, said, "Jeno has been virtually irrepressible over the years. It doesn't matter whether he's hustling garlic and bean sprouts or selling a concept of free enterprise—he simply never lets up. That's the bottom line on Jeno...that's why he's become a millionaire a hundred times over. You can love Jeno, or you can hate Jeno, but you can no more deny him than you can deny a gale-force wind on Lake Superior."

Although Curt Carlson and Jeno Paulucci are among the more successful of the Minnesota business leaders to emerge since the end of World War II, there are dozens, perhaps even hundreds, of other impressive businessmen who have contributed much to keeping the state an industrial leader, but it would be impossible to list them all.

Likewise, it is impossible to mention all the companies, or even all the industries, which have come alive in Minnesota in the past

30 years. The state has become a leading producer of medical products, for instance, with the nationally famous Medtronic, Inc., a heart pacemaker manufacturer, leading the way, and more than a dozen different companies also involved. The plastic industry has attracted several companies to Minnesota, and the new snowmobile industry was born in the northern part of the state and opened up an entirely new type of manufacturing.

Before the 20th Century comes to an end, it's almost a certainty that at least another dozen Minnesota companies will be joining the list of billion-dollar corporations. These include, besides those previously mentioned, promising firms such as Toro, Josten's, Modern Merchandising, Nash Finch, Pacific Gamble Robinson, Economics Laboratory, American Hoist, Gelco, Deluxe Check, Republic Airlines, Apache and Munsingwear.

Undoubtedly, there also will be giant companies disappearing from the Minnesota scene, some, perhaps through failure, but most likely through acquisition by outside firms which will move present facilities out of the state. The real challenge facing Minnesota today is whether the opportunity still exists for new businesses to begin, to grow and to eventually replace companies leaving the state. Critics of the present Minnesota business climate claim that opportunity is disappearing.

Bill Norris, the founder of Control Data, has said that conditions in the state in the late 1970s would make it impossible for an entrepreneur to start a corporation the way he started Control Data.

In at least one respect, there's no question that Norris' fear is correct. When he started Control Data, Norris and the other founders took their original stock, used it as collateral to borrow money to buy more stock, and then used that stock to borrow money to buy even more stock, and, somehow, managed to keep the company from going bankrupt. Under today's stringent state laws, a founder must place his original stock in escrow with the state of Minnesota, prohibiting him from using it as Norris and his group did.

There also are dozens of other rules, regulations and laws making today's business owner much less likely to survive those universally tough first few years. Under today's governmental ground rules, it is unlikely that men like James J. Hill, Frederick Weyerhaeuser, Cadwallader Washburn, George Draper Dayton or any of the pioneer entrepreneurs could have built their empires.

Minnesota faces another major problem in business expansion

in that many large corporations based here are building new plants, not in the state, but in other areas where the business climate is more attractive. Compounding this is the almost complete lack of major outside corporations starting new operations in the state. Not since IBM opened its computer facilities in Rochester, Minn., has a major non-Minnesota company started a sizable enterprise in the state.

During the decade of the 1970s, Minnesota-based corporations built more than 125 manufacturing facilities in other states, involving more than 30,000 jobs. Some of these would have been located out of the state regardless of the business climate here, but many could just as easily been constructed here if governmental interference and the tax situation were improved.

Minnesota today is among the highest tax states in the country. It has one of the costliest workmen's compensation programs in the nation, among the most strict industrial safety codes and environmental protection programs. Government officials and some legislators argue that Minnesota's business climate is not as bad as critics say, but the important thing is that the vast majority of businessmen in the state feel drastic improvements must be made to keep the state an industrial leader.

In 1978, the chief executive officers of 50 of the state's largest corporations formed the Minnesota Business Partnership with its main goal to improve conditions for business. Its main concern is not for favorable treatment for the giant companies here, but for more opportunities for small businesses to grow in the state. How much success this group will have remains to be seen, but the mere establishment of the partnership indicates that business leaders are concerned about the future of free enterprise in Minnesota.

Some educators today contend that the bulk of university students are turned off by business and are not motivated by money, although in an era of declining college enrollment, the nation's business schools are full and many have long waiting lists. All of the above observations affect Minnesota as well as the rest of the country.

While it is probably true that, due to government regulations, there will be fewer companies in the future obtaining their start-up capital from initial public offerings, there is no reason to believe that the future will not produce its share of Curt Carlsons and Jeno Pauluccis. And it seems very likely that Minnesota's many strong and well-managed corporations, whether publicly- or privately-held, will continue to grow and prosper, producing more jobs, larger payrolls and increased tax revenues. And in recent years there seems to have been growing awareness in state government of the difficulties that have been encountered in attracting new businesses and facilities to Minnesota.

So while the rough and tumble era of the latter decades of the 18th Century and of the early 19th Century will not be repeated, it seems likely that, except for the difficulty raising start-up capital through the stock market, the business future of Minnesota should continue strong and healthy, producing a growing number of giants.

Index

facturing, 9, 20-23, 54, 133, 145
Minnesota Mutual Life Insurance, 12, 43, 44
Minnesota Title, 4
Minnesota-Wisconsin Truck Line, 11
Mode O'Day, 124
Modern Merchandising, 166
Moore, Tom, 163
Morgan, J. Pierpont, 46-52, 54, 91, 104
Mosher, J.B., 26, 27
Munsingwear Co., 145, 166
Murphy Motor Freight Lines, 11
Murphy Transfer & Storage, 133
Nash Finch, 7, 166
National Cash Register Co., 153 154
National City Bank, 47
National German American Bank, 116
Nationwide Carriers, 11
Newell and Harrison Co., 129
New Prague Flour Mill, Inc., 16, 73
New York Stock Exchange, 48, 51
Nichols, J.A., 94
Norris, William C., 152-162, 166
North Central Airlines, 10, 30, 31
Northern Fire Apparatus Co., 147
Northern Malleable Iron, 133
Northern Ordnance, 146-150
Northern Pacific Railroad, 10, 30, 36, 42, 45-54, 59, 95, 104, 116
Northern Pump Co., 146-151
Northern Securities Co., Ltd., 52
Northern States Power, 12, 133, 138
Northfield & Southern Railroad, 10
Northland Foods, 164
Northland Milk, 7
Northrup King, 4
North Star Foods, 7
Northwest Airlines, 10, 24, 25, 26
Northwest Airways, Inc., 25
Northwest Bancorporation, 11, 133, 139-141
Northwestern Aeronautical Corp. (NAC), 146, 152, 153

Northwestern Bell Telephone Co., 112, 133
Northwestern National Bank of Minneapolis, 12, 140
Northwestern National Life, 44
Nuclear Data, 160
OCR Systems, 158
Oak Dale Farms, 18-20
Old Dutch Foods, 7
Oliver, Henry, 91, 96, 97, 104
Olson, Floyd B., 137, 138, 141
Onan Corp., 146
Ordway, Lucius Pond, 21-23
Osborn-MacMillan Elevator Co., 62
Osborn, Merritt J., 23, 24, 31
Owatonna Canning, 7
Owatonna Tool Co., 145,
Pacific Gamble Robinson, 7, 166
Pagel Pump, 147
Pagel, Theodore, 147
Paine, Parker, 40, 41
Pan-O-Gold Baking, 7
Paper, 133
Parker, John E., 152-156
Partridge, Elmer, 25
Paulucci, Luigino Francesco (Jeno), 162, 165-165, 168
Peavey Co., 7, 58
Peavey, Frank Hutchinson, 58, 63-65, 90
Peavey, George Wright, 65
Peavey, James, 64
Pike, Zebulon, 107
Pillsbury, Alfred F., 70
Pillsbury, Charles A., 30, 58, 65-71, 90, 98, 121
Pillsbury Co., 5, 6, 29, 30, 58, 68-71, 73, 139, 145
Pillsbury, Fred, 70
Pillsbury, George A., 66, 70
Pillsbury, John Sargent, 30, 58, 66, 70, 121
Pillsbury-Washburn Flour Mills Ltd., 70
Poppin' Fresh restaurants, 6
Polar Star Milling Co., 15, 16
Preston Associates, 158
Prince, George, 141
Printing, Inc., 110
Processed Potatoes, 7
Puffer, Paul, 24